The
ELLEN
MCCALLISTER
Story

The
ELLEN
MCCALLISTER
Story

KAREN Y. TYE

Pennsauken, NJ
Published 2021

This book is a work of fiction. All the characters, situations, and locations are a product of the author's imagination or used in a fictitious manner.
Printed in the United States of America

ISBN: 978-1-66781-824-5
eBook ISBN: 978-1-66781-825-2

Library of Congress Control Number:

ACKNOWLEDGMENTS

I am grateful to Vicky McGath, whose skill put the story on paper and into a manuscript; Karen L. Olson, copyeditor extraordinaire; Patrick Johnston, technical advisor; friends Inez, Fran, Jeady, and Patsy; and my daughters Krista and Jillian—for all their time, help, and encouragement.

Dedicated to Kymery Tyelyn Carlson

March 30, 1961, to January 4, 2019

Contributions to research for pancreatic cancer are appreciated.

CHAPTER ONE

Ellen sat on the back step of the family summerhouse, enjoying the garden her mother had spent years landscaping. She thought it looked beautiful but knew that if her mother were sitting here now, she would be dreaming of something different or more interesting. If her dad were here, he would remind her of the time, energy, and money it would cost—and that moving trees and shrubs was not the same as moving furniture in the living room. Smiling to herself, Ellen recalled how her mom would paint a mental picture of what she had in mind, and before she knew it, her dad would buy the picture and start adding his own details. Her smile faded as once again she recalled why she was here and how much she missed her parents. It wasn't summer vacation time—it was prepare-the-house-for-sale-so-the-estate-could-be-settled time.

Now time to get back to work—packing the keepers and pricing things to sell. Many items showed their wear, but since this was the place Ellen McCallister had spent the better part of her childhood summers, memory or sentiment was tied to nearly everything. As hard as this was, she was also dealing with the end of her thirty-year marriage and the fact that her architect husband wanted to keep the house he had designed and built. That house had always seemed to be more his than hers or theirs. However, leaving it would mean that she would have to find a place to live once she sold the summerhouse.

"One solution would be to move to the coast, fix up the summerhouse, and live here," she thought. "An advantage would be not having to ship all the things I want to keep and, of course, not going through the process of buying or renting a new residence. At this point, the familiar seems more comfortable than the alternative.

"But do I really want to leave Indiana and live in Land's End full time? Most of the old friends I enjoyed each summer have moved on just as I have, and all those professional and business associations that make everyday living simpler would have to be reestablished. A dentist who would understand why I'm so frightened at every appointment, a beautician I could trust, a florist who could make an arrangement without putting a big bow on it, a handyman, someone to help with the yard, a veterinarian since Shazey will surely be staying with me . . . the list seemed endless. Maybe staying isn't a good idea. Damn Jason!" she thought. "His timing couldn't be worse."

She shook her head and said aloud, "Stop worrying. Get this exhausting job done. Take one step at a time!"

Friday arrived with the sun shining brilliantly through the bedroom window. No rain was a prayer answered. It meant she could remove the plastic that covered the tables filled with things to sell, and she could put out the estate sale signs.

She also took a little extra time dressing. She wanted to make a good impression on the community she might . . . maybe . . . decide to live in. She pulled on a sweater and around her waist buckled the old fanny pack she had found upstairs, thinking it would serve as a money belt.

No sooner had she put out the signs and folded the last piece of plastic, when the first car stopped in the driveway. A sprightly woman about her age walked up into the yard and called out "Hello! Are you Ellen, Mary's daughter?"

"Yes, Mary was my mother."

"I'm Anna Thomas. I was sorry to hear about your parents' accident. I so enjoyed visiting with your mother during summertime. She gave me great gardening advice."

"I'm glad to meet you, Anna. Are you looking for anything in particular?"

"I've been thinking I'd like a round hassock—about thirty inches or so—or maybe an old table that I could cut down and use as a coffee table. I'm pretty handy at repurposing things."

"Mom had a table about that size. Would you like to take a look? It's up on the porch."

"Thanks, I'd like to check it out."

As they walked across the yard, Anna said, "I recall seeing many of these items in your parents' home that are now for sale. It makes me feel nostalgic. Ellen, what are your plans for your family's summerhouse?"

"I'm not sure," Ellen replied. "There are pros and cons both for selling and keeping it." Then remembering that her mother had often mentioned a friend by the name of Anna, she decided to share some of her concerns for moving full time to the coast.

"I can understand why this is a big decision," Anna said. "It certainly was for me when I left the Midwest. Now I'm really glad I decided to move. Why don't you stay for a few months and see how it goes? If it begins to feel like home, you'll know what to do."

"Good advice. And thanks for the suggestion. I don't have any time constraints, and I could use the time to investigate the financial aspects. No need to rush into anything. Well, here's the table—what do you think?"

After checking its stability and settling on a price, Anna said, "I'll take it. And I hope you'll stay in our little community. I know a good contractor. If you're interested, I'd be glad to introduce you. I'm very happy with the little house he built for me. I'll give you my address if you'd like to come out and see it. I always like showing it off."

"That's very kind of you," Ellen replied.

"No problem. I'm happy to help Mary's daughter."

Ellen carried the table out to Anna's car and thanked her again for the invitation to visit. By now the yard was filled with people looking for a great buy they couldn't resist. Little girls who were thrilled with her mother's old costume jewelry. Tourists who couldn't get enough of everything "beachy." Men her father's age interested only in tools and fishing gear. And women looking for antiques, canning jars, and old towels that could be cut into cleaning rags. Even though it was difficult to part with certain things, Ellen found it gratifying to hear how much shoppers admired the items or needed them to replace something broken or lost. From her customers' stories, Ellen felt that she was beginning to know some of the full-time residents of Land's End.

— —

By five o'clock, Ellen had just enough energy to pack up what was left and call the thrift store to haul it away. She found a bottle of Malbec in the pantry, uncorked it, and was about to fall into her dad's old office chair, when the doorbell rang. Walking toward the door, she recognized a customer who had been at the sale earlier that morning.

"Hi," he said. "I'm George Houser. I bought the floor lamp you had for sale—which, by the way, works perfectly in my office." Then, offering her a warm, wonderful-smelling box from the local pizzeria, he added, "I thought you might be hungry and too tired to go out or prepare something to eat."

"I'm starving!" Ellen said. "I'll even eat the box—unless there is something better inside."

George laughed and replied, "The Dish does a pretty good job. It's their simplest variety—five cheeses." Then he added, "I didn't know if you might be vegetarian."

"All cheese is just fine. It will be great with a glass of wine. Would you care for some? We could sit out here on the porch," she suggested.

"If you're not too tired."

"No question about it—I won't lie. I'm tired. But food delivered to my front door will revive me! Please sit down and I'll get you a glass."

A moment later, Ellen returned with a glass, the bottle of wine, and a roll of paper towels. "Sorry, all out of napkins. Hope you like red."

"I actually prefer red wine, thanks. So how did the sale go?"

"Couldn't have been better. Estate sales are a good way of getting rid of things you no longer can use. My parents accumulated a lot of things during the time they spent here."

"Are you planning to continue using the house as a vacation destination?" George asked. "I heard from your neighbor, a friend of mine, that your home is in Indiana."

"That's a question that has been keeping me awake lately," Ellen replied. "To sell or to keep? Besides all the emotional ties, I also have personal issues to consider."

"For what it's worth, my advice is, take your time. I'm sure you'll figure it out."

"That reminds me of some advice another person gave me today. Maybe I'll stick around for a while—see how it would feel to be a full-time coastal resident."

"It's not a bad place to call 'home.'" Handing her his business card, he said, "But if you have questions about selling, I might be able to help. I've had a real estate office in town for several years."

"Well, then tell me. How is the real estate market doing? Is our economy strong enough to support purchasing second homes?"

"You probably know that summer is the best time to sell vacation property," George replied. "However, we're beginning to acquire more full-time residents in Land's End than ever before. Many retirees seem to find the slower pace of living more to their liking, as do young couples raising families."

"That's good information. I'd like to hear more—perhaps another time, when I haven't been managing a yard sale all day." Laughing, she added, "By the way, do you entice potential buyers as well as sellers with great pizza?"

"Only if they are tired, hungry, and might enjoy a glass of red wine," he said. "Being pretty and hospitable helps, too," he whispered to himself as he was leaving.

Ellen washed, dried, and put away the glasses and then headed for bed. Before turning off the light, she leaned against the doorframe. With fresh eyes, she surveyed the familiar kitchen. There was no doubt—whether she stayed or sold, a lot needed to be done to this room.

Exhausted was hardly the word to describe how Ellen felt. The few moments it took to get ready for bed seemed like an eternity—but falling into bed was like a long-awaited gift. A prayer of thanksgiving and a plea for guidance quieted her mind for sleep, which came almost before she uttered, "*Amen.*"

— —

It was Sunday morning, Mother's Day! Ellen lay in bed wondering, "What are my children doing today, missing the opportunity to celebrate with their own mother. I know Jenny will be calling, and there will be talk about the divorce and her dad. Maybe I can see how she feels about her mother living on the coast permanently. On the other hand, that might be too much for either of us to deal with."

Sunday in Ellen's family meant church. She remembered one a few miles out of town that she and her family had attended. "Church could be just what I need this morning," she thought.

She enjoyed the drive. The abundance and variety of foliage. Some about to bloom; others, like the shore pines, bending architecturally to the ocean wind. But it was always the smell of the sea that penetrated her senses. It gave her a feeling of peaceful anticipation.

Seeing the church sign, she wondered, "Will I take it all for granted if I become a full-time resident of Land's End?"

"I surely hope not," she said aloud.

As she entered the narthex, an usher handed her a pink carnation and wished her a happy Mother's Day. In the sanctuary, the choir began singing "God Himself Is Present." Everything looked and sounded so familiar that Ellen thought, "It almost seems like Mom and Dad should be sitting in their usual spots in the third row on the right. If I should start crying, perhaps I should leave right now."

But then a kindly gentleman whispered, "Good morning, ma'am. Welcome to Trinity" and handed her a bulletin.

Ellen found an empty seat on the back pew. Glancing up toward the altar, she thought she saw George Houser in the choir. Somehow, seeing him brought her back to the present. She smiled and opened her hymnal.

After the last hymn and blessing, she said hello to a few people she had met at the estate sale. As she prepared to leave, she heard a familiar voice calling out, "Hey, Ellen! Wait a minute—I thought I saw you from the choir."

"Good morning, George. Nice to see you again. Have you been a member here for long?"

"I joined when I opened the office in Land's End. My home is about a mile south, just across the Henderson Bridge. Say, I usually go to The Kitchen after the ten o'clock service. Quite a few members meet there. Would you care to join us?"

"That's a nice idea. Perhaps another time. I'm expecting a call from my daughter sometime today that I don't want to miss. So, I'd better get going."

"I can understand that," George said. "'Another time' sounds like you might be thinking of staying or at least keeping the summerhouse—yes?"

"We'll see," she replied as she unlocked her car door.

Ellen passed The Kitchen on her way home and decided by the number of parked cars that it must be a very popular place on Sunday mornings. "If

Jason, Jack, and Jenny were here, that's probably where they'd be going now," she thought. Suddenly, a feeling of abandonment overwhelmed her.

When she got to the house, she lingered in her mother's garden, not wanting to go inside. But hearing the phone ring, she hurried up the steps, thinking it was Jenny. Ellen was surprised but not disappointed to find that the caller was Anna. Anna's cheerful voice and invitation for coffee and fresh strawberry scones quickly brightened Ellen's mood and disposition. She could call Jenny later if she missed her call.

Anna's little house was as charming as she was. Its French door, large skylight, bright color, minimal décor, and comfortable furniture made the combination living room, dining room, and kitchen appear open and welcoming. Anna had already turned the occasional table into a functional hassock. With a small bouquet of nasturtiums on a simple tray, it was the perfect place to rest one's feet and set a cup of coffee or glass of wine.

"Your hassock looks wonderful," Ellen commented. "And it fits perfectly in this space. You're very creative, much like my mother. I can imagine her doing something like this."

"So, you think she would have approved?"

"Absolutely! I like doing things like this, too. But I don't have the talent my mother had."

"I'm not sure how much is talent. It's more a lack of fear of failure. For me, it's usually just a matter of getting an idea, doing it, and hoping for the best. If it doesn't work, I try something else."

"Well, looking around your home, it certainly seems to work for you."

"It works for things like hassocks," Anna said. "But building a house takes a professional. I gave my contractor some ideas. With his talent and knowledge, he knew how to execute them. That reminds me, have you made a decision about your summerhouse?"

"Sort of. It needs a lot of work, regardless of what I do. So, I'm going to stay for the summer, as you advised. I'll get a builder and repair and remodel as if I were going to stay in Land's End permanently. By the time it's completed, I'll hopefully know what is best for me."

Anna said, "See, that's how it's done—worry a little, dream a little, think a lot, and figure out what you need and what you want to spend. Then, if you want, I'll have my contractor, Al Kaskala, stop by, and you can decide if he's someone you could work with."

"You are a wealth of helpful advice and information. I'm so glad you happened to need a hassock. Just one more thing." Ellen pointed to her hair. "See this? It desperately needs a cut and some color. Do you have a suggestion?"

"Yes, I do," Anna said. "I've been going to Andrew's on the Sound for quite a few years. I don't know of anyone who doesn't like them. Now come take a look in my little greenhouse. Maybe we can find a few berries for you to take home."

After finding just enough for her morning cereal, Ellen took them to her car. Then, turning to address Anna, she said, "You know, I was feeling pretty down when I drove out here, but after our visit, I have the beginning of a plan for the house, a possible builder, and the name of a beauty salon. And I've had the best scones I've ever eaten—plus more berries for tomorrow. Thank you. And thank you for being my mother's friend. Somehow, I don't feel as alone as I did an hour ago."

——— ——

Ellen was cleaning the strawberries and putting them in the refrigerator when the phone rang. This time it was Jenny.

"Happy Mother's Day, Mom. How are you doing, and how did the sale go?"

"The sale was a success but totally exhausting. Sold nearly everything, so there wasn't much to clean up. I met a lot of very nice and interesting people, so it was a win-win all around. Good weather too—no rain!"

"Looking around my house and seeing what could be—even should be—discarded makes me tired," Jenny said, "so I can imagine all you had to do at Gran's and Grandpa's summerhouse. Having it done must feel like a real accomplishment."

"Yes and no," Ellen replied.

"What do you mean?"

"Just that one thing leads to another. Now that the house is uncluttered and beginning to be cleaned out, I can see a lot of disrepair. I think I'll have to stay in Land's End at least for the summer to manage the renovation and probably some remodeling."

"But can you do that without Daddy?"

Ellen found that irritating. "Jenny, I may no longer have a husband, but I still have a brain! I'll just have to hire someone who can help me. In fact, I already have a lead on a contractor."

"Sorry, Mom. I didn't mean to imply that you couldn't manage. It's just that Dad is an architect and builder. He has always taken care of that sort of thing—at least, I always count on him for anything that I want fixed."

"And I'm sure he's glad to help—but someday he may not be available, and then you'll have to figure it out for yourself."

"Speaking of Dad not being available, can I ask—how are you doing with this divorce business?"

"Of course you can ask. We can't let it become an elephant in the room to be walked around." After a long pause, Ellen continued. "Sometimes I still get mad—really mad. His timing couldn't have been worse. However, lately I've been trying to apply your grandfather's philosophy: 'Life is what it is—deal with it—one situation at a time.' It seems to be working. I don't get bogged down as often, and I'm accepting of new ideas. Like today—instead of thinking I had to attack the next thing on my to-do list, I gave myself a day off and went to that little church near the beach that we used to attend with your grandparents in the summer. Then I visited a friend of Gran's and had the best strawberry scones. I'm feeling more relaxed than I have in a long time."

"You sound great, Mom. One thing at a time, huh? I'll try to remember that. Did you get the recipe for the scones?" she questioned.

"That's not my problem today," she replied. "But tell me, how's your brother doing? Is he coping any better?

"Jack's in a sad place. He can't handle knowing his father is some dirty old guy who would rather have a young girlfriend than an old family."

"Stop it, Jenny!" Ellen blurted. "Your father is not some dirty old guy!" When she regained her composure, she added, "Jack needs to stop thinking and talking that way."

"Well, what should we think!"

"I'm sorry, Honey. I can't tell you and Jack what to think or how to feel. I can only share what I think, if that would help."

"It might. Anything would be better than keeping it all to yourself—as though we were not involved."

Ellen detected sarcasm in Jenny's voice. Trying not to overreact but to be truthful, she said, "When your father and I married, I thought every building he designed was brilliant, and I lavished him with praise. I could not find enough superlatives to describe his amazing talent. Then he designed and built our home, which I loved. Shortly after that, you were born, then Jack. Life was full. I always wanted a family, but children do consume a lot of one's time. As you well know now that you're a mother. And I have to admit, I had less interest in poring over blueprints."

"Isn't that pretty normal, Mom? Marriage, children, new interests—we change."

"Yes, but my new interests excluded him. In fact, it was just about that time that Gran and I opened the dress shop. Moving on should not mean moving apart. Your Dad and I became more like roommates than a married couple. Consequently, when Sonja joined the firm and she admired and complimented his work the way I had, it was no wonder he was attracted to her. Besides, she could talk architecture, while I talked fashion. The length of women's skirts was about as interesting to him as the cost per square foot of a building was to me."

"You're scaring me, Mom. This could happen to a number of my friends—even to me. So, what do we do?"

"I'm not an authority, but I know you can't take each other for granted. Try doing more things together. Play golf or tennis, run a marathon—anything."

"Yuck! I hate to sweat!"

"Oh, Jenny—then swim. Join a bridge group, or a book club. Remember when Gran and Grandpa took up Asian cooking?"

"Then it was Mexican, followed by Italian cuisine."

"The point was that they enjoyed doing it together. That's what your dad and I didn't do.

"Okay, Mom. I think I get the message. Thanks!"

"And thank you. I needed to talk. I needed to hear what I've been thinking, so I could make an honest judgment about my feelings. Knowing I wasn't going to be judged made it a lot easier to say it out loud."

"Mom, I love you. I'm so proud that you trusted me enough to share your feelings. I'll try not to be so hard on Dad and also to help Jack."

"Sounds like we're both in a better place," Ellen replied.

"I think so. Maybe if you're going to be at the summerhouse for a few months, could I come and spend some time with you?"

"Of course! I'd love to have your company! Just let me know when. Bye for now, and please greet Jack and kiss my granddaughter for me. Love you." Ellen hung up the phone.

CHAPTER TWO

This Monday, unlike any other day in the past several months, Ellen didn't have a to-do list. Not that she didn't have any number of projects to tackle, but nothing absolutely had to be done today. So, for the first time in a long while, she lingered over her morning coffee and Anna's delicious strawberries.

Then she slipped on a pair of gardening shoes and wandered around her mother's garden, warmed by the bright glow of spring sunshine. Newly fallen cherry blossom petals blanketed the path, reminding her of her childhood. She used to imagine that the beautiful pink and white path was a wedding aisle, and she was the bride.

Ellen's parents had done most of their own gardening. That had never been Ellen's forte, so she had no idea what needed to be done this spring. She couldn't bear the thought of losing any of the plants because of her lack of knowledge. She would feel guilty for letting her mother down. So, she had to find help, preferably the person her parents had hired in the last few years to do the work they no longer could. She hoped the name would be in her parents' address book or gardening journal.

Her dad's desk would be a good place to start. His files were as organized as his office in Indiana—everything in alphabetical order except for one in the back of the drawer with a file labeled "Odds and Ends." In it, Ellen found an assortment of advertisements ripped from magazines, theater bills, church bulletins, wedding and death notices, funeral programs, and group photos taken at various picnics and celebrations. Nothing there had to be dealt with immediately. Ellen began searching through the files for what to throw away and what to keep.

A. Appliances: manuals for her parents' latest purchases for the summerhouse. Keep.

B. Bank: already taken care of.

C. Contributions: throw except for current year.

D. David: who or what was David? Laughing, Ellen remembered when her mother had named her walker "Fred." She wondered whether her father had named something, too. But she also found a newspaper clipping of a David Holiday standing in front of an espresso stand at Driftwood Cove, a picture of two young women, and an envelope addressed to her father from Georgia Holiday. The file contents left her with more questions than answers. Keep.

E. Earthquake: a few pamphlets on survival tactics for when the "Big One" hits. "That would be good to review," she thought. Keep.

F. Fireplace: a keeper.

G. Garden: a landscape plan, receipts for plants, some business cards, including one stapled to the file with a gardener's name. Definitely a keeper. She could cross that task off her to-do list.

All the other files were empty except J and R. The J file was filled with pictures and letters from Jenny and Jack. Keep.

H. R. Remodeling: clippings and drawings (some from Jason) that her parents had probably planned on using at some future date. Considering that her grandfather had built the summerhouse in 1930 as little more than a beach cabin, she knew it had been a residence in progress for many years. And now she was about to add her own ideas. Keep.

Ellen pulled the Odds and Ends and R files to look through more carefully that evening. Several drawers remained—her favorite ones because they held all the things a young girl on vacation needed for an art project, a thank-you note, or just to make a list of things to remember, like books she wanted to read, places she wanted to go, materials she might need for her next project or party.

Her father had kept colored pencils, felt-tip pens, glue sticks, Scotch tape, large and small paper clips, scissors, rulers, a small level, a couple of different sized magnifying glasses, paper hole punch, and paper—all kinds of paper. Any kind of paper you might need—anything from card stock to red, yellow, green, and blue Post-its, copy paper, nice stationery, and little tablets that were just fun to look at.

She remembered how generous her father had been with his magical stash. He had only one rule: "You have to ask because it isn't yours to take—only mine to give." One day when she asked, he told her where it was. "Open the drawer and help yourself." He trusted her! She was growing up. What an extraordinary day!

Now, as an adult, she had to deal with the loss of her parents all by herself and take responsibility for things she knew nothing about—and didn't want to know. She missed them both so much. She could hear her dad say, "Go ahead, Honey, take the tablet. You might need it for your grocery list." So, she did, then closed the drawer, leaving it just as he had.

Her thoughts were interrupted by a call from Anna. "I'm coming into town to do some shopping and have lunch with a friend. Would you like to join us at Wanda's?"

"I'd love to. I need to do some grocery shopping anyway, and I'd like to wander around Land's End and check out some new businesses and stop in at my old favorite bookstore. See you soon!"

As Ellen got ready, she wondered whether Claire Brown still owned The Bookstore. Mrs. Brown always suggested books that would hold Ellen's interest but not keep her awake at night. Mrs. Brown called it "summer reading." Then she would add books that she called "a little meatier—just because it's summer doesn't mean you can stop learning."

Ellen quickly found the restaurant from the directions Anna had given. Wanda's was a cozy, inviting restaurant with round tables for four arranged next to street-side windows. The tables were set with colorful placemats and matching fabric napkins. On each table sat a bouquet of wild daisies. Ellen felt like she had been invited to a private home—not a typical restaurant.

Anna and her friend, who were already seated, beckoned her to join them. To Ellen's surprise and delight, she recognized Anna's friend as Claire Brown, The Bookstore owner.

"I just learned that you two have been acquainted for a number of years," Anna said.

"Yes, Mrs. Brown kept my nose in a book quite a number of summers."

"So good to see you again, Ellen. Are you still an avid reader?"

"I still have a couple of books going most of the time."

"One fiction and one a little meatier, I hope," Mrs. Brown said.

"You remembered!" Ellen replied. "I was planning to visit The Bookstore after lunch. Now that the estate sale is over, I'm hoping to have a little free time."

"I was sorry to hear of your parents' accident," Mrs. Brown said.

"Thank you for the lovely card and letter. I was surprised—actually, in awe—by the number of cards and personal notes from people in Land's End."

"Your parents and grandparents had property on Blackberry Lane for many years. I doubt there are many locals who didn't have some contact with them. They were more than just summer people."

"Changing the subject, you probably didn't even know that Claire sold The Bookstore this winter," Anna said.

Looking at Mrs. Brown, Ellen replied, "No. What made you decide to sell?"

"I'm getting old, and I'm looking forward to seeing some of the places I've been reading about all these years. So, when opportunity knocked, I said yes, grabbed my book list, and walked out the door," Mrs. Brown said.

"Well, aren't we the life-changing group," Ellen said. "Anna has built a house, you sold your business and are becoming a world traveler, and I'm . . . getting a divorce and may be moving to the West Coast."

"And renovating an old house," Anna added.

"That's right. I'm going to need the name and phone number of your builder. I've been known to wheel a paint brush and pound a nail when the situation called for it, but that's the extent of my carpentry skills."

Hey, let's order. I'm getting hungry," Anna said. "I'll give you Al Kaskala's number after we eat."

The three wome continued to enjoy each other's company as they dined on fresh crisp salads loaded with crab, probably harvested the night before, and topped with Wanda's home-made Louie dressing. "One of the perks of staying in Land's End," Ellen thought. "And how delightful to already have two friends, Anna and Mrs. Brown." Ellen felt as comfortable with them as with a pair of old shoes, as the saying goes.

The Bookstore was just a block away, so Ellen headed in that direction. When she entered, the sound of a bell brought back memories from years ago. It reminded her of the first time she bought a book.

"The library," she thought, "was a great place to spend a rainy afternoon, but it didn't compare to a bookstore where I could buy a book that would become my own. One that I didn't have to return in two weeks. I could underline sentences that excited me or even make notes in the margins in case I was impressed or disagreed with the author."

Surveying the interior of The Bookstore, Ellen noticed a lot of changes. It no longer had that old Andrew Carnegie sound and smell. Even the comfy but worn upholstered chair had been replaced with colorful Eames egg chairs. She missed the old but loved the bright, welcoming new décor and the additional lighting.

Moments after Ellen entered, a young woman greeted her. "May I help you?"

Ellen guessed that she must be the new owner Mrs. Brown had mentioned. "I used to spend many happy hours here during summer vacations with my parents years ago. I was just admiring the changes you've made. Everything is so cheerful and inviting."

"By the way, I'm Judy Holiday, the proprietor, researcher, and barista. Those little pedestal tables are convenient in case customers want to enjoy an espresso while looking over a book. Is there anything in particular I can help you with?"

"Well, considering what I'm embarking on, perhaps a book on contemporary beach cottages would give me some ideas to consider. Also, a good fiction book to get my mind off the project from time to time."

"Our building and home décor subjects are quite limited," Judy replied. "Your money might be better spent at Fred Meyer. They have a great selection of periodicals. But if you have a particular designer in mind, I could see if there is anything I can order. However, I just finished Jodi Picoult's *Leaving Time*. It's a mystery with a twist that held my interest from cover to cover."

"I've always enjoyed Picoult, so on your recommendation, I'll take it, and thank you for the tip on Fred Meyer."

"While I get your book, would you like an espresso? You can try out one of our new egg chairs."

"Thanks, but I just had lunch and still have several stops to make before I go home. But could you give me directions to Andrew's on the Sound? I've been told they do good work."

Andrew's on the Sound was immaculate, and the appearance of Mark, the stylist, reflected well on the quality of the salon, so Ellen felt comfortable there. Next to good, professional service, Ellen's priority in a beauty salon was cleanliness. "A messy salon is as despicable as a messy doctor's office," she thought.

After scheduling her much-needed haircut, Ellen walked back to her car, feeling more optimistic about giving Land's End a try. She mentally reviewed her accomplishments: cleaning out the house, meeting some more locals, renewing an old acquaintance, buying a book to start reading, and scheduling a salon appointment. Now for grocery shopping and a light dinner— then she could call it a very good day.

—— ——

Judy Holiday was right about the large selection of magazines at Fred Meyer. After thumbing through several, she chose one specifically dealing with kitchens, another that emphasized space and storage, and finally one with such a pretty cover that she couldn't resist taking it home to spend more time evaluating its contents.

With magazines in hand, she pulled out her grocery list and noted how short and basic it was. Everything would probably fit in two shopping bags. "Not at all like back home," she thought. There her weekly shopping included the needs of two adults, one dog, the possibility of family and neighbors dropping in, and maybe a church potluck or a weekend dinner party. But what really caused her to pause was the word *home*. "Is Indiana still home? Will it always be home? Or can I really make a home here in Land's End by myself, no husband, no Jenny, no Jack? It's going to take a lot more praying to come up with an answer," she thought.

George, the "pizza delivery man," was heading into the grocery store just as Ellen was putting away her cart. "Hi, Ellen," he called. "How's it going?"

"Very well. I've been checking out the town. Land's End has grown substantially since I came here with my parents each summer, but I like that it still has a small community atmosphere. I had a delicious lunch at Wanda's and met the new bookstore owner. She's no Mrs. Brown, but she certainly has the interior looking fresh and warm. She gave me some good advice, too."

"On selling or staying?" he asked.

"No, neither. I'm still on the fence about that. I've decided to remodel as if I'm going to stay, though."

"Good idea! With that in mind, the house will not only be more saleable but more comfortable if you stay."

"Could we have lunch or coffee soon? Then you could fill me in on what potential Pacific Northwest buyers are looking for?"

"How about Friday around noon? I usually leave that time open.

"Great! Would noon at Wanda's be okay? I've got an appointment at one thirty that afternoon."

"Wanda's at noon is fine and an hour should give us enough time. See you then."

Another item to cross off her to-do list. "Am I getting too obsessed about my to-do lists?" she wondered. "Probably, but that's okay. It's just a way of staying on track and getting things done—a sign of accomplishment. Good girl. You got that done!"

CHAPTER THREE

After her day in town and then putting away groceries, Ellen was too tired and not hungry enough to prepare anything to eat, so she grabbed a drumstick off the roasted chicken she had purchased. She poured a glass of Malbec and sat down on the back steps to read the magazines. Not having to care for anyone else, she could relax and enjoy time for herself.

Home? Going *home? Homesick? Home?* She couldn't get the word out of her head. "What does *home* mean?" she wondered. "It must be more than a place to put your stuff. Maybe it's something you miss so much that it makes you sick to be away."

She didn't miss the house in Indiana. For that matter, she didn't miss much of the stuff inside it.

She did miss Jenny and Jack and her crazy book club, however. But that was people. She wanted to know about the physical building. If she could figure out what made a house her home, then she would know how to make the summerhouse her Land's End home where she could live.

The more she thought about it, the more complicated it became, so she started looking through the kitchen magazine, pulling out pictures she liked. She quickly turned the page if its contents didn't appeal to her. She knew she would need storage for dishes, pots and pans, and food. The flooring would need to be replaced, along with the countertops, of course. Cabinets would be a big expense. What size and how many? And there were so many styles of cabinets and hardware. Color? She had no problem with that. She knew very well what she could live with and what she could not.

Then the big questions: Will the kitchen have to be expanded? Will an addition infringe on the living room or her mother's garden? How much will all this cost? "Stop worrying," she told herself. "These are questions for Al Kaskala. I need to focus on the basics. What will make this *my home*?"

The concept she kept coming back to was "a place for everything and everything in its place." Maybe that's what a home would have to be for her. The certainty of knowing where to find things gave her a feeling of comfort, even safety. Definitely peace of mind. Not just the certainty that the cutlery was in the right-hand drawer next to the refrigerator but also that her hand sprinkler and pruning shears were in the basket on the bottom shelf in the closet next to the back door.

"Wow!" she said out loud. "I think I've got it." Not just storage but specific storage that suited her needs and that potential buyers could use for their own needs. Realizing that she knew where to start made her feel calm and confident. While drawing mental pictures of a pantry, kitchen, and laundry, she was startled when the phone rang.

"Hi, Jack. So good to hear your voice."

"How are you doing, Mom?"

"Really good at the moment."

"I had a visit with Jenny over lunch. She said that you have to do some work on the summerhouse. Having any problems along that line? Maybe I could help. You know you really have to be careful hiring a contractor and signing contracts," he said.

"I know, Jack. Remember I was married to an architect. Building of any kind was a major part of our conversations."

THE ELLEN MCCALLISTER STORY

"I didn't mean to insult you, but you did say 'at the moment things are really good.' Dad doesn't need me right now, so maybe I could fly out, have a little beach time, and be a sounding board when you need one."

Ellen remembered that when Jack got an idea in his head, he couldn't let it go. She responded, "It's not exactly beach time yet but nicer than Indiana weatherwise. So, if you just want a change of scenery, please come. I've been missing you."

"But you did imply that there was nothing I could help you with right now—at the moment."

It's just an expression, Jack. I was just speaking philosophically about the definition of a *home*. I'm sure it's different for everyone. For instance, could you live comfortably in your neighbor's new house?"

"No, I don't like a lot of wood paneling and hardwood flooring. I guess you might say I'm more of a 'shiny black-and-white tile, painted walls, and big windows' kind of guy."

"I wasn't referring to décor. When you called, I was feeling very good at the moment because I had just concluded that for me, my home was where I could put my hands on anything I owned at a moment's notice. It would give me a sense of security, even peacefulness."

"Hmm. Is that why you're not fighting Dad on this divorce business—because he seldom put anything away?" Jack asked.

"Oh, I doubt that any one thing is the cause of a marriage breakup, but always searching for something can be very frustrating, so adequate and purposeful storage will definitely be my priority."

"Wow! You're deep, Mom! Really deep. Most people start with cash availability and number of bathrooms and bedrooms."

"I suppose," Ellen agreed. "However, they probably haven't just cleaned out a very old family summerhouse and are currently unsure where they will be laying their head a year from now."

"Exactly. Just say when it will be good for me to come out and help with all practical— and maybe emotional—decisions."

Taking a deep breath as she searched for the right words, Ellen stayed calm. She replied, "It will be good to see you, Jack, but when you give advice, remember it's my life and my home we'd be talking about."

"Of course, Mom. I've been working with a couple of Dad's clients, so I know how important listening is to understanding what the client really wants."

"I didn't mean to insult you either," Ellen said. "It's just that working with a relative, let alone your mother, could be tricky, and I want our time together to be pleasant."

To assure his mother but not take all the responsibility for a congenial visit, Jack quickly replied, "We'll work to make that happen. How about if I make reservations for the middle of next month? I'm sure you'll have some ideas and maybe decisions by then."

"I certainly hope so. Then you can meet my contractor and catch up on my plans. Let me know your arrival time, so I can have some Sam Adams and jerky on hand."

"Some crab would be great, too." Jack laughed.

"And some steamers or oysters, too?" Ellen added. Laughing, she hung up the phone.

CHAPTER FOUR

Ellen woke excited to start the morning. Kicking off the covers, she swung her legs over the edge of the bed. Her feet found the old loafers she had forgotten when her family left Land's End the fall she started high school. The next summer, the loafers didn't suit a teenager's style, but she recalled conversations with her parents and Land's End neighbors about needing to have good footwear by her bed in case of an emergency, such as broken glass due to an earthquake. So, the loafers had survived years of vacations, and once again she put them to use.

Today she didn't need a to-do list. It would take most of the day to review her thoughts about storage, find examples in magazines, and tear out pictures for future reference to show George and the contractor she would hire. The situation was complicated by not having committed herself to being a full-time resident or a vacationer or a seller. Since Ellen was now in her fifties, she had pretty much determined what she could live with and what she could not, but what would sell in a beach community was up for grabs. So, having lunch with George could be helpful.

By late afternoon, she had gleaned as much information as she could. She filed pictures and articles that her parents had saved in a folder. And she paper-clipped articles from magazines and some of her own ideas and drawings and questions. The wastepaper basket was full and the desk clean except for the folder marked "D" for David. With no serious intent, she opened the D file, where she found the newspaper clipping of David Holiday and the envelope addressed to her dad. Something about him looked familiar, but whatever it was didn't register.

Being tired and hungry, she replaced the picture and took the folder to the kitchen. For dinner, she decided to prepare a bowl of homemade tomato soup and a grilled cheese sandwich. She loved her mother's recipe. A tablespoon of finely chopped onion sautéed in a couple tablespoons of butter, and a tablespoon of flour—let it cook for a little while. Then add a cup of milk. When it begins to thicken, add two freshly peeled, seeded, and chopped tomatoes. Add a pinch of baking soda and salt and pepper to taste. So easy and so good. Make it better by tossing in a handful of garlic croutons to float on top. With a grilled cheese sandwich, it couldn't be better.

While the soup simmered and the sandwich grilled, she got out David Holiday's picture and the letter addressed to her father. She thought, "The letter will surely give me some idea why Dad kept the picture in his file."

Dear John,

It was nice to see you this summer, and as I promised, I did ask David if he wanted to meet you. Remember, I told you David and my husband are very close, so I wasn't surprised when he replied, "No, I already have a father, and I don't need another one." Please don't be hurt. Be thankful God gave him two good ones. Fortunately, one he has known most of his life, and one gave him great genes but was too young to handle the responsibility of fatherhood. Have a good year and maybe we'll see each other next summer.

Best wishes, Georgia Holiday

Unlike the night before, Ellen didn't sleep well. It seemed that no matter how hard she prayed or tried to concentrate, she couldn't keep her mind on track. Thoughts whirled around like a windstorm.

Was David Holiday her father's son? Her brother? No! No! Half brother? Did her mother know him? When was he born? Before they were married—or after? An affair! "Oh, Mom, how awful for you. Would Dad really have done that to you? Maybe I'm making a wrong assumption. Maybe Dad had investigated someone for a friend and the letter was meant for someone else. He wouldn't have hurt Mom that way—or could he? They didn't always get along. Mom always wanted more children and Dad didn't." She remembered that. "Arguments! Who was Georgia Holiday? Did she live in Land's End? What about Judy Holiday, The Bookstore owner? Was she related? She seemed to be about the same age as Jack and Jenny. Jack and Jenny? What about them? *Oh, dear God, what am I to do about this?*"

One thought led to another question to another thought until she was crying and wishing desperately to talk to her mother. And getting mad at her father, not for having a son she didn't know about so much as leaving a letter for someone (her) to find. Near dawn she finally fell asleep only to wake up with a throbbing headache and, of course, no resolve to the situation in which she found herself.

The next few days were a blur. The thought of an unknown brother and all the uncertainties it entailed made working on the remodeling project almost impossible. Plus, she was really feeling the pressure to have some constructive ideas and questions to share with George on Friday. In frustration, she decided to get out of the house, go to a movie, or better yet, drive to the beach.

The ocean had so much to offer. The smell of salt air, the sound of water lapping on the shore, and of course the anticipation of finding something the tide had coughed up during the night. Thoughts of the ocean were already clearing David Holiday from her mind.

Leaving Land's End behind, Ellen began to notice blossoms on the native dogwoods and tiny white buds on the blackberry vines. Tucked among the vines, a sign advertised

New Beach Home Development

Scheduled tours available

One mile south on Shore Pine Rd

"Great!" she said aloud. "Just what I need. Isn't it amazing how God provides when you need it!" David Holiday was not on her mind anymore.

Ellen drove into Harbor Shores and was immediately glad that she had decided to take a look. She drove through the parking lot, stopping at the entrance to a group of sherbet-colored cottages with metal roofs of a coordinated color. The abundance of native shrubs and trees surrounding the houses made her think that Harbor Shores would be just as inviting on rainy days as it currently was on this spring morning. Noticing an office sign, she decided to check in for a tour.

An office employee informed her, "No one is available until noon on weekdays, but tours are given all day on Saturdays and Sundays. However, since you're on site, feel free to walk around the development." She gave Ellen an attractive brochure that described the amenities and prices for three different floor plans.

"How many houses have been sold?" Ellen asked.

"Several—and as far as I know, they're all going to be used as vacation properties."

"Thank you for the information. I'd like to walk down to the beach and will probably be back this weekend to take a tour."

On the way to the beach, Ellen compared the houses to hers in Land's End. Although the summerhouse was not large, it was certainly bigger than these. "It would be useful to see how they used their square footage," she thought. "Tomorrow, George might give me some tips on what to look for."

The Harbor Shores developer had built wide stairs down to the water. Ellen paused there to savor the beautiful view, the outgoing tide, the warm sun, and the inviting smell of the ocean. Totally engrossed in the beach environment, she relaxed. Not one thought of David, Jason, Jack's pending visit, or the renovation project crossed her mind. It was as though her mind had been scrubbed clean, unblocked, and released from all her to-do lists and problems. She laughed as she pointed her finger toward the sky and figuratively crossed them all off an invisible to-do list. Having a clear head now felt unreal but yet very pragmatic.

On that note, Ellen decided just to enjoy the rest of the day. Walking down to the beach, she whispered, "*Thank you, God.*"

On Friday morning, Ellen grabbed the file of notes and pictures she had compiled. "Prioritize," she thought. "I have only one hour to eat lunch and discuss the vacation house with George before my appointment at Andrew's on the Sound. Most of all, I need assurance about the best way to begin the remodeling plan and what would work best in a summerhouse where storage is prime."

Wanting to appear businesslike, she donned her best jeans, a clean Henley, and her go-to-everywhere blue blazer. She arrived at Wanda's comfortably early and picked a private table, hoping not to be interrupted by any of George's friends or business associates. When the waiter arrived, she ordered a cup of clam chowder and the shrimp salad that Anna and Mrs. Brown had raved about when they had lunch together a week ago.

No sooner had the chowder arrived than she heard George say, "Hi, I see you picked one of my favorites. Wanda makes the best."

"That's what my friends said. Sorry for not waiting, but I wanted to have some lunch and then discuss how and when to begin my renovation project before my appointment at Andrew's. At this point, I'm not sure which is more important to me. But some of this hair has got to go, or I might lose my mind."

"Good thinking . . . about not losing your mind. Give me a minute to order some chowder, and then we can get right to your renovation project."

While George waited for his lunch, he browsed through the file of notes and pictures Ellen had brought. He asked, "Do you like to cook and garden?"

"Love to cook," she replied, "but I'm not the gardener my parents were. Other than some weeding and planting of spring annuals, I'd probably have a gardener. I'd hate to mess up my mother's expert work."

"What about harvesting our abundant seafood?"

"I spent a lot of summers here, remember?" Ellen said. "I can't see living on the coast or selling to anyone who wouldn't want to take advantage of the clams, oysters, crab, etc. But even if I stay, I wouldn't be a boat owner. If a buyer wanted a boat, there is room in the garage for a small one and the paraphernalia that goes with it."

Laying down the file, George said, "Ellen, I can tell you have given a lot of thought to this renovation. Regardless of which avenue you choose, it's pretty clear that storage is most important to you. I'd suggest you start with that. My experience has been that a kitchen can make or break a sale, so that's where I'd put my money. Have you decided on how much money you want to spend? Have you found a contractor?"

"Yes. No. Maybe," Ellen answered. "Hopefully, I'm going to meet Anna's builder, Alvar Kaskala, next week. Anna speaks highly of him, and after seeing her little house last Sunday, I could tell he is not afraid to try something new if the plan calls for it. So, I guess if I knew what the summerhouse is worth, I might have a better idea how much to spend."

"Good. I know Al quite well. He's helped me on a few houses that needed some repair or updating, so I know he can do renovations as well as new builds. Why don't I come over after church on Sunday, take a look at the house, do some measuring, and check some comps. Early next week, I can give you a real estate appraisal. That is, what I could sell the house for as is."

"That would be wonderful, George."

"Say, if you're going to be in church Sunday, how about having brunch at The Kitchen after services?"

"Okay, that's a good plan," she said. "And now I really have to go." She gathered her papers and laughed. "The next time you see me, I'll be the gal with a new haircut.

CHAPTER FIVE

"Hi, Ellen," Mark called. "Help yourself to a cup of coffee or something cold. I'll be with you shortly."

Ellen poured herself a glass of water from a pitcher that appeared to have just been replenished with ice and lemon slices. It was a pleasant surprise and added to the relaxed, welcoming atmosphere of Andrew's on the Sound.

She settled into a comfortable chair and immediately recalled her conversation with George. She was pleased how quickly he had picked up on her need for adequate and purposeful storage and then correlated that need with remodeling the kitchen in terms of cost. It was also reassuring that he knew Alvar Kaskala and respected him as a knowledgeable builder.

Lost in her thoughts, she wasn't aware of Mark standing in front of her until she heard his voice. "Good to see you, Ellen. I've been looking forward to becoming more acquainted. Ready to get that haircut?"

"Am I ready! I've been ready for over six weeks. Fortunately, Anna Thomas gave me your name, so here I am."

"You've got great hair. Are all those curls natural? Are you thinking of something new as far as style goes?"

"All natural," she replied. "Lately my days have been very full since coming back to Land's End, and my thoughts have pretty much revolved around essentials. Usually, though, I'm up for anything as long as it's easy to take care of. Got any ideas?"

"Not at the moment, so let's go back to my station for a shampoo. I'll mess with it a little, and we'll see what comes to mind. Sometimes when life throws a lot at us, it's a good time to try something new, and sometimes it's exactly when we should take a breath and embrace the old tried and true."

"I like the way you think, Mark," Ellen said, as she sank into another comfortable chair, feeling very safe and secure. She was glad Mark did not pursue a conversation as she was totally engaged in relaxing and letting Mark make all decisions until she saw the results.

Before she knew it, the sounds of the scissors and blow drier stopped. She could see Mark's reflection in the mirror. He was staring at her as he turned the chair from side to side. Then he said, "This may not be the final decision, but considering you have a lot going on now, how about just a good trim. Then to make it even easier, I'll give it a tight bob on the back. For most of my clients with short haircuts, I've found the length of their bangs and hair covering their neck creates a lot of anxiety until they can get back to the salon."

"I'd definitely fit in that group of clients. Hair in my eyes and tickling my neck is like a cat on a hot tin roof."

Then, a bob it is. By the way, what has been filling the life of Ellen McCallister these days?"

"Oh, just renovating a sixty-year-old family vacation house and getting acquainted with Land's End as a single adult after thirty years of marriage. Every day seems to be filled with consequential decisions, plus surprises popping up here and there."

Mark was the kind of beautician who wanted to know his clients but only to the extent they wanted to be known. So, casually he said, "Well, that would certainly fill anyone's plate. Hope getting a fresh haircut will cross one of those things off your list."

"It certainly makes me feel better," she said.

"And getting to know Anna Thomas has to be a plus. I love that lady. Isn't she a wonder!"

"I'm very fond of Anna. She's one of those people that what you see is what you get. You never have to wonder what might be behind what she says. Besides, she knew my mother. That in itself makes her special."

"Well, I don't know if my next client who's walking through the door knew your mom, but she's a very special citizen of Land's End, too."

"Could I meet her?" Ellen inquired.

"Of course. Georgia, come here and meet a newcomer. This is Ellen McCallister. She's renovating an old family home on Blackberry Lane. Ellen, I'm happy to introduce you to Georgia Holiday."

CHAPTER SIX

All the way home, Ellen thought about meeting Georgia Holiday. She wondered, "Does Georgia know that John Underwood was my father? She didn't act or sound shocked but did take a deep breath when Mark introduced me and mentioned that I'm remodeling an old house. That alone could create some attention in a small resort town, and as Mrs. Brown said, my mom and dad were well known, so it was unlikely that the Holidays weren't aware of their accident and death."

Ellen thought that Georgia was an attractive black woman about her mother's age, and she seemed kind and receptive to meeting a newcomer.

"But do I want to know the woman who my father was intimate with and had a son?" Ellen asked herself. "Then what about David? Would he want to meet me? Would I want to know him? He didn't want to meet Dad. Would I feel rejected if he didn't want to meet me, or would it even matter?"

"What about Jack and Jenny? Would they want to know him? What about his being biracial?" She didn't think they had ever shown any signs of racism. On the other hand, the subject had never come up in the family.

So many thoughts kept getting mixed up with making decisions about the remodel. "How many shelves do I need to accommodate my books? Do I really want to keep the wedding china? And where would I put it if I kept it?

Uncertainty like this made her wonder, "How am I going to resolve my feelings about a sibling I've never met? What does this say about my father and my feelings toward him? One thing is certain—I can't pretend that it never happened and that I never knew anything about it. I need to talk to someone. But who? Maybe my best friend since college, but she's in Indiana, and the subject is too long for a phone call and too emotional for an email. Besides, I don't want my personal life floating around up there in the cloud. Jenny? No, too soon. George? I like him a lot, but too personal. And he probably knows the Holidays, so that wouldn't be a good idea. Anna? Hmm. That could be perfect. She knew my mom, and she's easy to talk to. She doesn't seem to make judgments without good reason.

"I'll give it a little more thought. One of the nice things about being in a good marriage is that you always have a trusted person to talk over difficult situations with. But if you're not, you don't."

By that evening, she had decided to call Anna and ask if she could come by tomorrow morning because she needed to talk to someone.

"Of course, I can," Anna said without hesitation. "You sound worried. Anything I can help with now on the phone?"

"No. It's too long and drawn out. I just need to get a few things off my chest so I can focus on the renovation more clearly."

"Then I'll see you tomorrow. How about some scones to go with coffee?"

"Anna, you're a dear. See you about nine."

Rain pounding on the roof woke Ellen from a deep sleep. She liked the sound. Gathering the quilt under her chin, she couldn't help but feel grateful for a good roof and a cozy warm bed when it was raining so hard.

The room she had been using since coming to settle the estate was the one she had occupied as a child. However, with all the renovation planning, it had occurred to her that if she kept the summerhouse, she would need room for guests. Jenny and her family would need this room and Jack's old room too. She wondered whether she could ever comfortably take over her parents' room downstairs. Once when she was sick, she had slept in it, but now it reminded her that they were not alive.

"Get up," she encouraged herself. "Get the coffee on and lay a fire to warm and cheer up the living room before Anna arrives."

Anna drove up during a break in the rain and came running up to an open door. Ellen shouted, "Come in—quick before it starts to pour again. I've got a fire in the living room, and coffee and mugs are there."

"Bless you! That's some storm we're having. So glad I have my little greenhouse. Strawberries would never have survived this downpour."

"But I'm sure your scones would be good even if you didn't put anything in them," Ellen replied.

"My friend Annette gave me the recipe, and they are pretty good with just a drizzle of frosting. But enough about scones. Pour me a cup of coffee, please, and let's get to what's bothering you."

"Okay! You know I've been in quite a quandary about whether to stay or sell. I've been leaning more toward staying lately. However, now something else has come up that gets in the way of my thinking and making plans to remodel and stay."

"What's that, Ellen? Care to share?"

"I asked you to come because I felt comfortable sharing with you." Ellen began reciting the events of going through her father's desk, discovering the letter from Georgia Holiday, and then meeting her at Andrew's on the Sound.

"I'm so confused. I know nothing about David Holiday. A half brother? Did my mother know about him? I don't know how to proceed with this information. Do I share it with my children? I'm not sure. How would they feel about their grandfather? How do I feel about my father? I've never wanted to talk to my mother more than I do now. I don't think I care so much about David

Holiday as I do about Dad saving a letter for anyone to find. Why didn't he talk about him?" Finally, Ellen's tears began to flow.

Anna walked across the room and gathered Ellen in her arms. "Go ahead and cry—cry it all out. You've been through so much lately. That horrible accident, then your parents' death, the stress of settling their estate. On top of that, the divorce and the end of a way of life you've known for the past thirty years. Then finding that letter! I can't imagine how you have been able to handle it all. Cry, Ellen. Go ahead and cry! Sometimes there is nothing better than a good cry. When you're finished, there will be time enough to work on solutions. For now, just cry."

And so she did.

Finally, out of exhaustion, the tears and sobs stopped, and Ellen was able to speak. "Do you know Georgia Holiday? If you do, what's she like? Do you know David? Does he live here in Land's End? Do you think I should meet him? We do have the same father. I can't pretend this didn't happen, but you know in the letter, she said he wasn't interested in meeting his father—the biological one. Maybe he already has a sister. What should I do about this, Anna?"

"Oh, Ellen, I'm not sure, but I have to agree with you. It's never wise to ignore reality. On the other hand, I don't think you have to do any more than you want to or are ready to do. Time is on your side."

"But do you know them?" Ellen persisted, "or anything about them?"

"I know that Georgia is on the city council. She always supports the city pool, so she gets my vote. I know that David is a businessman. I understand he is quite successful. He has two daughters. One has an espresso business at Driftwood Cove, and the other bought The Bookstore. Word has it he financed both businesses. I've also heard that he prefers to spend a lot of time with his fisherman father on his boat. That's about all I know."

"Georgia mentioned in her letter to Dad that David and his father were very close, so I'm not surprised they spend a lot of time together, and there was a picture of a man who could certainly be David at the stern of a large boat.

But wouldn't you think he would be curious to meet his biological father?" Ellen asked.

"Yes, but curiosity is only one component. Maybe he was afraid to meet him. Afraid that your father wouldn't like him, or he wouldn't like your father, or afraid that his color would be an issue. He could even think that the man responsible for his conception didn't care enough about him to help raise him or was dismissive about his mother. Anger and fear can muster up a lot of negative feelings. To be fair, we probably shouldn't be too rigid in our thinking or conclusions."

"You're right, Anna. I've just been wound up in how all this affects me. I haven't considered how the situation had to affect them."

"Don't be too hard on yourself. This was dropped on you like a bombshell at a very difficult time. Give yourself some time. It's a wonderful healer and often opens our minds to new ideas like discovering that sibling your mother may have always wanted for you."

"Anna, I appreciate you! You've helped me to see that there is much more involved here than just my feelings. And you are absolutely right. I don't have to do anything about that letter right now. A good cry followed by some time and prayer is my best solution. Plus, listening to the counsel of a trusted friend."

"And a project that needs attention," Anna added. "I see a folder here marked 'Renovation.' Got anything you'd like to show me?"

Starting to feel better and wanting to apply herself to something constructive, Ellen eagerly accepted the opportunity to discuss her ideas. "Anna, here are some drawings I think might work. What do you think about these pictures?"

So, the morning went from problems to tears to consensus to relief as Ellen began to feel that progress had been made. She realized that worry and fear were not going to make the situation go away any more than not caring about them. Right now, her priority was to contact Anna's contractor.

Alvar Kaskala picked up the phone on the second ring. In reply to Ellen's inquiry about his availability, he said, "I'm giving myself a long weekend to relax, but I don't have any commitments for some time. I'm glad to explore a new project."

They agreed to meet next Tuesday.

——— ——

After the serious rainstorm on Saturday, Sunday morning, in every sense of the word, was a new day. The sun rose in all its glory, making the wet leaves shine. When she opened her bedroom window, breathing in the fresh spring air, she was reminded of a favorite prayer, "This is the day the Lord has made, let us rejoice and be glad in it." With resolve to let the Holiday situation rest, she smiled and said, "*Thanks, again, Lord.*"

George followed Ellen home after brunch with church friends at The Kitchen. He took some measurements and got pertinent information on the plumbing, heating, foundation, and so on. He reminded Ellen that after he did some comparisons of homes that had sold in the last few months, he would probably be able to give her a report by mid-week. Then he said, "Why don't you come into town next Wednesday night, and I'll take you out to dinner. You can look over the comps I found, and I can give you my suggestion on what I could sell the house for."

"Thank you. That would be nice. Let me know the time and place," she replied. "I'm meeting Alvar Kaskala on Tuesday, so I might have some idea of how much I will have to spend to have the house updated."

"Sounds like things are progressing. Eager to see you then," he said in parting.

——— ——

Alvar arrived exactly when he had promised. This was a quality she admired. Being courteous was an act of civility that made communication easier, she found. Once again, she was grateful for Anna's suggestion to consider him for the renovation.

Watching him walk up the front porch, she noticed that he was tall and casually dressed, and he walked with a slight limp. He appeared to be about 35, and for some reason, she was glad that he was neither younger nor older.

"Come in, Mr. Kaskala. I've been looking forward to our meeting.

"Please call me Al, and may I call you by your given name? The sooner that

we can forget formalities and you can show me your project, the sooner I can help you make it a reality."

"That's a good idea. Please call me Ellen. Let's sit at the table, and I'll show you what I've been working on. Would you like some coffee? Cream? Sugar?

"I don't know anyone from Finland who would turn down a cup of coffee. I'm Finn, so thanks and no thanks. Black!"

"A man of few words: good," she thought. "Friendly but doesn't waste time."

Holding up one of the folders, Al said, "I see you've been doing a lot of preparation for our meeting. I like that. It shows me you're serious about the undertaking. Leaning back with arms folded across his chest, he gave her his full attention. "But this doesn't tell me why you need help."

"I'm serious but still not totally committed to staying in Land's End. That's why I need your help," Ellen explained. "How do I get the things I want but not overdo it in case I end up selling the house?"

"Do you think there's anything you want that would keep a buyer from buying your remodeled house?"

"I never thought of it that way. I was just thinking of cost."

"So, maybe I need to know what Ellen needs to make it her home?" Al questioned.

"I know the answer to that one. Not long ago, when I struggled over the question, I realized that a place for everything and everything in its place makes me feel comfortable and at home. Sounds kind of boring and rigid. Maybe that's who I am." With that, she frowned.

"No, these drawings don't show me a rigid person. On the contrary, an efficient and imaginative description would fit better. By the way, these drawings are good. Have you built before?"

"Sort of," she replied. "My, ah, husband . . . you might as well know . . . soon-to-be ex-husband, is an architect. Can't tell you how many floor plans I've pored over. I guess the process rubbed off a little. You'll notice measurements are missing."

"We all start with design. It's when we know the site and the budget that the work begins. We have an expression in Finn, *sisu*. There's no translation, but most often it's defined as "guts." I prefer "perseverance.""

"I like those words—*efficient, imaginative, perseverance, guts.* With your help, I may be able to pull this project off. A third-generation family summerhouse becomes Ellen's home. Sounds good!"

"I'm sure we can. The plans you drew and the old ones give me the location of many of the things I need to know. I'll take them all home and see how much I can include without infringing too much on your living space."

"Or too much on mother's garden," Ellen said. "I did measure from the northeast corner of the house to the dogwood. It was my mother's favorite tree. We can't disturb it."

"We won't break a branch," he assured her.

"And you'll give me an estimate of the cost and time it will take?"

"Of course. Decisions can't be made without that information. Give me a week, and we'll get together again and make some final plans. Okay if I walk around the back on my way out?"

"Yes, certainly. I'll join you."

CHAPTER SEVEN

Ellen concluded that there was little she could do about the summerhouse until hearing from George and Al. Not wanting to think about the Holidays, she called the gardener mentioned in her parents' file.

He told her, "I'm a retired farmer—an old man who loves to dig in the dirt. I'd be happy to help you any way I can."

While waiting for him to arrive, George called. "Hi, Ellen. I've completed the appraisal. Would you like to go over it while we have dinner tomorrow night at the Vista House? I can pick you up since you live between my office and the beach."

"Thanks, that would be nice," she replied. "I've never been there, but my parents spoke highly of it, and I'm anxious to learn what value you came up with for the summerhouse."

"Good! I look forward to seeing you again. About six tomorrow, then?"

"I'll be ready!" Ellen immediately began wondering what she brought from Indiana that would be suitable for a business social dinner at the Vista House.

Recalling his words *seeing you again* and *eager* made her wonder whether there was more to his attention than just getting a listing on her house. It had been a long time since she had even considered that a man might be interested in her other than as Jason's wife or Jenny or Jack's mother.

Shaking her head and laughing, she said, "You're crazy, Ellen McCallister. Get back to reality." About that time, Mr. Green knocked on the backdoor and introduced himself, asking "What would you like me to do?"

"Hello, Mr. Green Jeans. I'm so glad you could come and help me out. I never developed the skill or had the talent like my mother on gardening. Maybe we could just walk around, and you could tell me what needs to be done."

"Mr. Green Jeans—hmm—you must have watched *Captain Kangaroo*! He was my son's favorite."

With a big smile, Ellen said, "I'm so glad you knew where that name came from. My mother and I watched his show together when I was a child. It was one of my favorites, and she enjoyed it, too."

"Your mother was an excellent gardener. I enjoyed working for and with her. Each fall before your parents left for the winter, she gave me a list of things to do like clean up the fall leaves, prune the hydrangeas, clean out the annuals that were done blooming, and generally get ready for spring."

"What you're saying then is that there's not much we need to do right now."

"No! There is always something you can do in the garden. Things happen in the winter. See those broken branches? They need to be cut off, and the ferns need to be cut back. Those dead fronds don't look very pretty, and I'll need to know what annuals you like so I can figure out the best place to plant them, along with any changes you would like to make."

"Mr. Green, I'm going to leave the choice of annuals up to you. Whatever you and my mother did before is just fine with me. As far as changes go, I'm not planning any. I may be selling the house. New owners may want to make changes, but I hope they will just leave it as my parents left it."

"I hope so, too," Mr. Green said. "But, you know, we all have our favorites. Even Mother Nature sometimes likes a change. See these little primroses? Did you know they don't' like to stay in the same spot year after year?"

"I didn't know that," Ellen replied. "When would you have time to start? I don't want my mother's garden to look like she abandoned it."

"Let me finish putting in my vegetable garden. How about the first of next week? Speaking of vegetables, your mom and I often put in some greens and tomatoes along with the flowers. One time we planted a row of corn over there where the sun is shining by the garage. Looked darn good, too," he said as he walked away.

Watching him leave, Ellen said to herself, "You sure knew how to pick them, Mom. People that is, not just plants. I think Mr. Green Jeans and I are going to get along just fine."

— —

Time to shower and get dressed. George would be there in less than an hour. What to wear was no longer a big concern when she remembered how limited her current wardrobe was. The only suitable dress she had packed was a blue silk, spaghetti-strap sheath with matching jacket and silver-braided belt. The last time she wore it was to Jason's and her thirtieth wedding anniversary celebration. She remembered on that occasion thinking the jacket looked too matronly, so she chose a white cashmere shroud. But tonight the jacket would be perfect because it was always cool on the beach after four o'clock. Besides, even if she was fifty plus, she liked the way the belt showed off her trim waist.

George arrived about ten minutes late, which for some reason, didn't bother her too much. Perhaps because he was very apologetic and acknowledged that she looked especially pretty that evening. And it was quite clear that he had changed to a fresh white dress shirt and maybe even a new tie.

On the way to the Vista House, they talked only about real estate. "How is the market this spring as opposed to a year ago? Is the supply equal to the demand? What are buyers looking for?" Then, more to the point, "Where does my house fit in if I decide to sell?

The Vista House sat on a hill overlooking the Pacific Ocean. A winding road was bordered by the largest rhododendrons Ellen had ever seen. "Driving up in June must be overwhelming! Have you ever seen them in bloom? What color are they?"

"They're a red that becomes slightly pinker as they come into full bloom. I think you have one on the southeast corner of the porch."

"In that case, I'll get to see it. It was always through blooming by the time we arrived from Indiana."

If Ellen was awed by the drive up the hill, she was astonished by the size and elegance of the Vista House. The first floor was built of logs all the same size—huge! The second story was cedar siding. A covered porch ran the full length of the house with columns of logs supporting the roof. Guests could sit on Adirondack chairs and view the lawn until it fell into the ocean.

"Would you like a glass of wine on the porch while we go over the appraisal before dinner? I ordered their favorite label of Pinot noir. In this part of the country, they sort of frown on it if you drink any other form of red wine," George said.

"A glass of Pinot noir would be nice, thank you. I like it just as much as Malbec."

Moments later, a server arrived with the wine followed quickly by a charcuterie tray of shaved meats and cheeses and Parmigiano crackers that Ellen was sure had been made in the Vista kitchen.

Still amazed by the columns, Ellen asked, "How could they find so many logs all the same circumference?"

Laughing as he tried to mimic a French accent, George said, "Monsieur Louent owned a hundred acres in this area. When he downed a tree this size, he had it hauled to the beach and saved until he had as many as needed to build his dream house, which is now the Vista House."

"That was quite an accomplishment and had to take a while."

"And then he had to build it. I heard that took better than five years."

"And I'm fussing over a few months," Ellen said.

"I know how you feel. We live in an 'I want it and I want it now' culture, which reminds me, I think our dinner is ready. I just heard the dinner bell."

Noticing a quizzical expression on Ellen's face, George said, "I hope I haven't made a huge mistake. Since your parents had talked about the Vista House, I assumed you knew they only serve two seatings each evening and have only one menu. Our dinner is at a quarter after six, and it's crab-stuffed salmon tonight." Hanging his head in mock contrition, he asked, "So, will you still have dinner with me this evening?"

Pretending dismay and then laughing, Ellen replied, "You're in luck, Mr. Houser. I still haven't seen the value you put on my house, and it's a long walk down the hill, plus I'm hungry, and I can't imagine how amazing our dinner will be. Let's eat!"

The wine server brought their bottle of Pinot noir and ushered them to a table set for two by the window. The table, of course, had a white linen cloth and napkins with "VH" embroidered in burgundy. A fresh fir wreath surrounded a single tall white candle. Ellen was happy to be seated by the window and equally appreciated that from where she was sitting, she could see the enormous rock fireplace and grand staircase. She thought another five-star restaurant would have chosen fancy crystal chandeliers, which would not have suited the room better than the old schoolhouse-type fixtures.

"This is a wonderful room," she told George. "It's surprising how they have made it so elegant and still common at the same time. It makes me feel very comfortable."

"And speaking of comfort, have you noticed the sound, or lack of it?" asked George.

"Yes, isn't it perfect? Just the occasional clinking of china and murmur of people talking and listening to music. It sounds like what you would hear in a movie where people are dining and visiting with one another. But, George, do you hear that sound the servers' shoes are making? It's like they're saying, 'Don't worry, relax, I'm on my way. I'll take care of you. Relax and enjoy.'"

"You have quite an imagination, Mrs. McCallister. But I understand what you're describing."

Dinner was just as good as Ellen had anticipated. She and George never did look over the appraisal and only briefly mentioned her meeting with Al.

Even though they had spent several occasions together, Ellen and George hadn't shared much about their personal lives. However, George was not surprised to learn that Ellen would soon be divorced, and she was not surprised that George's wife was deceased. Neither felt any need to go into detail about how these major events came about in their lives. She did tell him, however, "The death of my parents is a hard pill to swallow, and making solo decisions about my life is difficult. It's hard to think of 'I and me' as opposed to 'we and us.'"

"I think that death and divorce have many of the same problems," George said.

Ellen agreed, explaining, "Jack, Jenny, and Jason and I all lived in the same town before I moved to Land's End. Consequently, our children were a daily part of our lives. They never held back regarding their feelings about the divorce."

"In our case," George said, "both our sons had been living abroad quite a few years before their mother died. Of course, they were saddened by her loss, but it didn't seem to have a huge effect on their daily lives."

After finishing their poached pear and melt-in-the-mouth sugar cookies, George and Ellen reluctantly left the Vista House. They talked the entire way to Land's End about the fantastic dinner they had shared. George said, "I loved everything about the crab-stuffed salmon."

"I enjoyed it, too, but my favorite was the wild mushroom risotto. The conditions on the coast offer varieties I don't think I could find in Indiana. Mushrooms there didn't leave that intriguing musty, but not stale, taste in the back of my mouth like the Vista's did," she explained. "And what about those poached pears? They must have used curaçao. My attempt at being grandiose was to sweeten whatever red wine I had on hand. Sometimes it was good; some-times not so good." She laughed, remembering those times.

"Your culinary skills exceed mine," George said.

"You haven't experienced my not-so-good efforts. But I'll accept flattery most any time."

They arrived at the summerhouse, and George walked Ellen up to the door and handed her the appraisal that had prompted the dinner invitation. "If you have any questions, be sure to call me."

Then he said, "I really enjoyed your company." And with a soft kiss on her cheek, he added, "I hope I can see you again soon. Good night, Ellen."

She unlocked the door and headed straight for her dad's old leather chair. Kicking off her heels, she fell into the chair and said out loud, *"Well, God, what do you think of that? Is that going to complicate a nice friendship? He's a nice man. I like him, but I'm still married. In fact, I still even feel married."*

Ellen began to relax. Feeling the warmth of the big old chair brought to mind the many times she would come home worried, concerned, even angry about something, and her dad would quietly hold her and not say anything until she relaxed. The chair, like a proxy, was doing that now.

Finally, she picked up her shoes, headed for the stairs, and whispered, *"We'll have to talk about this some more tomorrow."*

CHAPTER EIGHT

Ellen awoke praying, "Help, *I need help. Bless my sorrow and guide my decisions today.*"

It had been two days since their dinner together and the kiss goodnight. She studied the appraisal. As far as she could tell, there was no reason not to trust George's evaluation. She was still in a quandary as far as how much to spend, especially on the kitchen update. She wished there were a formula so that she could simply plug in some numbers and magically come out with an adequate and safe amount to spend. Of course, that was ridiculous as it wouldn't allow for the myriad situations that could occur.

Dwelling on the subject wasn't getting her anywhere until she thought, "This is exactly the type of situation Jack would love to offer an opinion about. I know he's in the office by now, so I'll call him."

"Hi, Mom. Glad to hear from you. Got anything special on your mind? I have a meeting with Dad and a client but have a little time to talk."

"Sounds like you're busy, so I'll be brief. I got a realtor's appraisal on what he could sell the house for as is. Now I need to figure out how much to spend on the update—especially the kitchen. Gran and your grandfather left me some money, but I don't want to spend it all on the summerhouse. Got any thoughts along that line?"

"I guess it depends on what you want to do with the house. Do you just want to spruce it up and sell it? Or are you still thinking about keeping it as a full-time residence for yourself?"

Not wanting to sound too decisive, Ellen said, "At least for now, I'm leaning toward staying. The contractor I'm hiring is bringing a plan and estimate next week."

"He'll probably have a suggested budget for items like kitchen cabinets, lights, appliances, etc. I'd suggest you start making a couple of lists, one for things you must have and another for things you can live without, like custom-made cabinets as opposed to prebuilt from a big-box store."

"Good thinking, Son! I remember doing that when your dad built our house. Thanks for reminding me. By the way, are you still planning on coming to the coast? Have you made reservations yet?"

"My schedule is still the same," he replied. "Planning on leaving in two or three weeks, depending on when the job firms up. I'll let you know. Now, I'd better get going. You know how Dad hates to wait, Bye. Good luck." His voice drifted off.

"Same to you. Thanks again. Bye," she said to a silent receiver.

Still holding the phone in her hand, it rang. The caller ID read "Land's End Real Estate. Not sure she wanted to talk to George yet or knew what to say, she let it ring again before answering.

"Hello, George. How are you today?

"Doing fine, thanks. It's a busy time of year, but I wanted to keep in touch. Wondering if you looked over the appraisal and what you thought. Any questions?"

"No. Just a little surprised at the prices houses are bringing in Land's End."

"Does that make you more interested in selling?"

"Not really. It does make me more comfortable about putting money into the remodel, though. Whether I sell or stay, I need to update the kitchen, and I know that's a sizable expense."

"It's a known fact that kitchens and bathrooms can make or break a sale. Or keep someone in their house."

"There are so many factors involved in where we choose to live. I told you Jason wants to keep the house in Indiana, so I have to find a place to live. Currently, I'm thinking it might as well be somewhere I already have roots."

"If you're talking about Land's End, I'm in favor of that. I'd be happy to sell your house but happier to have you stay."

There those words were again. Ellen wondered what might be behind them and how she should react. Hoping that George would understand, she responded in as noncommittal manner as possible. "It's always nice to make a new friend."

"That reminds me," he said, "there's a welcome-home potluck for the snowbirds after the late service. On Sunday morning, I have to finish some paperwork at the office. How about I pick you up on the way to church?"

"Oh, I don't think so, George. I'm sure you know how complicated things can get when your personal life is unsettled. I don't want to say or do anything that would give anyone in Land's End the wrong impression. You know that the divorce is not final, plus most of the time, I still feel like a married person."

"Ellen, I appreciate your candor. I'm very impressed with how you have managed all the hurdles in your life lately."

"It's a God thing, George. It's always a God thing."

"I'm sure you're right. In any case, I'll see you Sunday."

— —

Ellen had no sooner hung up the phone when it rang again. To her surprise and discomfort, the caller ID showed the name Georgia Holiday. Reluctantly, she picked up the phone, and with controlled uncertainty, she uttered a quick "Hello?"

"Hello, is this Ellen McCallister?"

"You have the right number," Ellen replied.

"This is Georgia Holiday. We met at Andrew's on the Sound last week. I've been wondering if your maiden name is Underwood and if by chance John Underwood was your father."

"He was."

"I read about your parents' accident and passing. I just wanted to call and offer my sympathy."

Not knowing how to respond to this person she knew but didn't know, Ellen simply said, "Thank you."

After an awkward pause, Georgia finally said, "I read in the local paper that the Underwoods' daughter Ellen was in town cleaning out the family summer-house in order to settle the estate. How are things proceeding? Are you planning on doing any remodeling?"

"It's a big job. I found a contractor who has some good ideas. I'm finding that helpful."

Another lull in their conversation. Then Georgia said, "I knew your father very well and would enjoy visiting with you sometime about him."

This time Ellen didn't hesitate. "I love talking about my parents. My mother and I were very close, but right now I have a lot on my mind—about the renovation."

"There's no hurry. I'll give you my phone number. Call whenever you would like to talk."

Hoping that Georgia would think she was referring to renovation, she said, "It takes a lot of time to figure things out in order to make good decisions."

"Of course. I look forward to hearing from you in the near future," Georgia replied. When the line went dead, Ellen put down the phone, got a glass of water, and went for a walk in her mother's garden. If anyone would have asked, she probably would have said that she just felt numb.

Shedding the numbness didn't come easily. Even when she woke the next morning, Ellen felt like a cloud was hovering over her; it couldn't decide whether to blow away or spew buckets of rain. She welcomed the most minute distractions. Anything regarding the renovation took more energy and time than she was able to give. And anything regarding the Holidays left her with a vague perception of . . . nothing.

Jenny called and talked briefly, leaving Ellen feeling disappointed. She had to postpone her visit until next fall. Jack had asked her to give their mother a message. He couldn't leave for at least six weeks. Jenny said that he would call and explain later.

It seemed like everyone's life was moving on—except hers. She didn't know whether to cry, have a pity party and eat a bag of chocolate chips, or call a psychiatrist. She decided that she was tired of crying. That many chocolate chips would only make her sick, and she didn't know whether there was a local psychiatrist.

While she sat staring out the window and praying (God always seemed to be available), she noticed Al measuring the distance between the garage and the house. When he put his tape away, he spotted her and waved. Aha! A distraction. So, she beckoned him to come in.

"Hi, Ellen. How are you doing?"

"I think I need to develop more sisu. Does God ever play into it?"

"From whence do we get our energy to persevere?" he asked.

"You're right! Say, is that a house plan you have rolled up there?"

With a big smile he said, "It is! And it's all for you. I liked your drawing so much I just made a few changes and added the measurements we needed. I thought you might like to spend a few days with it before we meet next week."

"Do you have some time now so we could go over it? I really need something constructive to think about."

"Let's get to work then."

57

Looking over Al's plans, Ellen realized right away that the storage in the back entry was missing. Had he forgotten how important the right kind of storage was for her?"

"I'm sensing you've lost your enthusiasm. Show me what's bothering you."

"I thought it would be important to have a coat closet near the back door where I could also keep some basic outdoor tools," she said.

"You're absolutely right. I was thinking I could build something like this." He showed her a drawing of a cabinet with coat hooks, a bench, and cubbies for baskets. Then he explained, "It would fit at the end of the hall and hold everything that would have gone in the closet, plus giving five more feet to be divided between the half bath and the laundry area."

"Of course! That's a much more efficient use of space. I love having a place to sit down and change my shoes or boots. I can hardly wait to see what other creative ideas you've come up with."

The rest of the afternoon flew by while they enthusiastically exchanged ideas and modified what had been a nearly perfect plan. The kitchen cabinets became open dish shelves, allowing for more light. A person working at the sink would then be able to view the garden. They added a closet for brooms and cleaning supplies at the end of the stairs. They laughed when at the same time they discovered enough room for Shazey's bed under the open staircase. Locating a place and changing their minds became the name of the game in positioning the refrigerator. Finally, they decided that the pantry was still the best place for it, but it would open into the kitchen area.

At last, with everything that Ellen could think of—from garden tools to place mats to supplies of batteries—she and Al leaned back and drew deep breaths.

Ellen asked, "Do Finns enjoy a glass of wine as much as a cup of coffee when a job is finished?"

"Or a cold beer if you have one!"

"You're in luck. I stocked up on Sam Adams for when my son gets here. I'm sure he won't mind sharing a few."

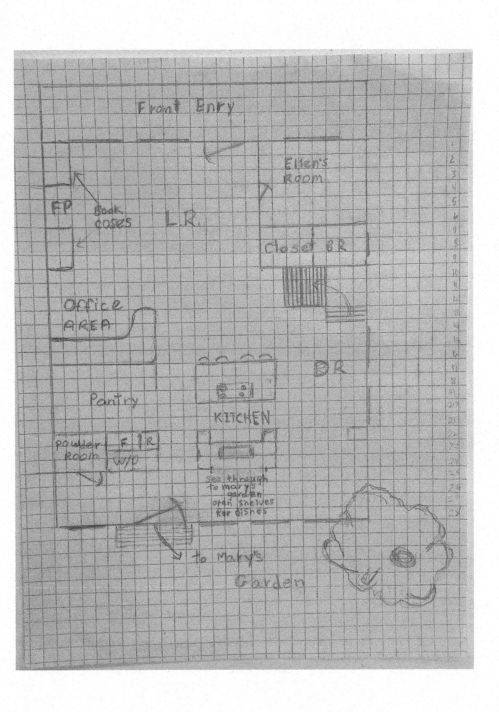

The SUMMER HOUSE

Mary's dog wood Tree

CHAPTER NINE

Several weeks had passed since Ellen and Al had finalized plans for the summerhouse renovation. Progress had been going quite well. Ellen had so many decisions to make that she rarely thought of the Holidays or her father's relation to them. When she did, she resolved her anxiety by saying a quick prayer. Then she was able to move on to the next order of business.

Anna and George usually checked in with her a couple of times a week, and she often had coffee or lunch with one or the other when she was in town picking up something for Al. She always mentioned, especially to Anna, how much she enjoyed working with Al. "He is such a good listener. If I do have a problem, it makes solving the situation easy."

Anna's response was typically Anna. "When he was building my little house, I noticed that, too." Then she added, "We would certainly have fewer problems if more of us defined *conversation* as 'talking and listening' rather than just 'talking.'"

◄ ►

Cost preyed on Ellen's mind. She thought lighting would be very expensive, but considering how crucial it was in the kitchen and pantry, she went with the recessed variety throughout the addition. Sometimes she referred to the list Jack had suggested she write and then would determine if the size and cost would fit the plan. Although she had some concerns, she did stretch the budget on the appliances but forfeited the big farm sink in favor of the same stainless with an attached drain board like she had in Indiana. Since the hardwood floor had been laid when her grandfather first built the house, she didn't feel confident about matching it with new wood, and anyway, tile might be easier to maintain.

Ellen and Al both liked the idea of concrete countertops but were having a hard time finding an experienced concrete counter specialist. Consequently, they didn't know if it would even fit in the budget. Other than the floors and counter, all the major decisions were not only made, but most of the material had been ordered, delivered, paid for, and in the garage—available when needed.

Today Al was starting on the cabinets while his crew finished drywalling. Ellen had gone into town to find baskets so that Al would know the measurements for the cubbies in the hall cabinet. She was also going to pick up a single burner hot plate to add to her makeshift cooking area. Processed microwaveable food was quickly losing its appeal, and cold cereal was still cold cereal, even if it was topped with a sliced banana.

After living in Land's End for a few months, Ellen seldom carried a cellphone. For one thing, she seldom needed one (no friends or family for whom she had to be at their beck and call), plus service on the coast was despicable. Lately, though, she tried to keep it charged and with her in case Al needed her to pick up something. Nevertheless, she was startled to see a text pop up from Jack.

"Hi, Mom. Problems solved. Reservations made. See you Friday p.m. Talk to you tonight." Jack.

When Ellen arrived home after picking up Jack from the airport, she saw Al's truck and realized that he was unloading the cabinets into the garage. She shouted, "Hey, Al! Come meet my son, Jack. I can hardly wait to see the cabinets!"

Brushing his dirty hands on his shirt and pants, Al eagerly reached out to shake Jack's hand. "So, this is Ellen's young architect. I've been looking forward to meeting you."

"And this must be the contractor extraordinaire who enjoys a Sam Adams on a hot day." Jack laughed but Ellen detected a slightly sarcastic tone.

"Only on a day that's been too long and hot, like today," Al responded.

To avoid any ruffled feathers, Ellen headed to the house. "I'll get you each a cold one and bring back a basket, too, so we can see how they're going to work. I'm especially excited to see the cabinet for the back hall."

Al said to Jack, "The one your mother wants to see is still in the truck. Want to help bring it in? I'd kind of like to see it in place, too."

Jack did not respond to Al right away but finally rolled up his sleeves. Walking to the truck, he muttered, "I guess I can."

Seeing it in place, Ellen clapped her hands, laughed, and hugged Jack. "It's just perfect! I love it! This is the piece that will take the place of a coat closet. Plus, it will give storage I need for tools, such as a hammer, pliers, screw drivers, and garden paraphernalia. Another basket will hold some nails, screws, mastic tape, or things I might need for hanging a picture or doing a small repair. Another I want for extra lightbulbs and batteries. Jack, look! Here's a spot for my umbrella and boots and a bench to sit on. Isn't it ideal? I'm so happy."

Jack extended his arm to shake Al's hand again, this time with the sincerity that earlier had been lacking. "Thanks. I haven't seen my mother so happy in a long time."

"These are the times when you realize you chose the right profession. No amount of money can take its place," Al replied. He gave Ellen's shoulder a friendly squeeze.

"Thank you, Al," Ellen said. "It's exactly as I hoped it would be."

"You had a lot to do with it, too, you know." As he climbed into his truck, he said, "If we are going to stay on schedule, we really need to make a decision about the countertops tomorrow."

And waving to Jack, he said, "Great to meet you. See you tomorrow."

Ellen grabbed Jack's hand and said, "Come on. I've got two—yes, two—cooked and cleaned cold Dungeness crabs and fresh sourdough waiting for us."

———

"Well, you're an early bird," Ellen said as Jack came in the front door.

"I woke up remembering how much I enjoyed Land's End when I spent time in the summer with Gran and Grandfather."

"And I was thinking how much they would have loved being here with you now."

"You miss them a lot, don't you?"

"Terribly! But renovating the house has been good medicine, which reminds me, Al will be here soon. We have to make a decision this morning."

"Yes, what was that all about? The countertops or something?"

"I really would like to have concrete countertops, but we haven't been able to find anyone in the vicinity who has experience fabricating them."

"Gosh, Mom, I may be able to help you."

"Really, Jack? I didn't know you had taken up laying concrete."

"No, but my fraternity brother Stu worked with his dad all through high school and since graduation from the university when he joined Anderson Tile and Stone. His father has been doing concrete counters for quite a while, and I know Stu has been helping. I don't know if he's your man, but it might be worth checking into."

"Any lead is a good lead at this point. Where are they located?

"That and timing may be a problem. Their business is just this side of Seattle. But Stu and I have been talking about getting together when I came out to see you."

"Maybe he could come to Land's End, see you, and do the concrete countertops."

"If he and his dad are comfortable with Stu doing the job on his own," Jack said.

While Ellen and Jack were discussing this possibility, Al had come in through the back door (a makeshift piece of plywood with a couple of strategically placed screws).

"Good morning. I didn't mean to eavesdrop, but I heard you might have a solution to our counter problems. Why don't you two drive up there? Jack, you could see your fraternity brother, and, Ellen, maybe you'll get the counters you've been wanting."

"Great idea, Al!" Ellen said. "And if Jack's fraternity brother can't do it, perhaps I'll find another product I like. Hopefully, then, we'll still be on schedule."

Jack called Stu and happily reported to his mother that he was free to see them tomorrow. The remainder of the day, Ellen and Jack spent preparing to leave Land's End for a couple of days. Ellen checked her to-do list for things needing her attention before she left. Al gathered information that Anderson Tile and Stone would need for the summerhouse renovation—mainly regarding concrete counters but also flooring for the kitchen and addition.

The next morning, Ellen had conflicting feelings. On the one hand, she looked forward to a road trip with Jack. On the other hand, she hated to miss any of the changes taking place in the house.

Over a cup of coffee, she and Al went over last-minute details. "You must remember the cost per square foot plus labor attached to a product," he told her.

"I'm more focused on maintenance and longevity, especially regarding flooring."

"I'll keep in touch," he promised.

"Thanks, Al. And I'll keep my cellphone charged."

Finally on the way, Ellen reminded herself that this would be a good time to forget about remodeling and concentrate on Jack. "So, how are things going now that you're a college grad working in your chosen field in your father's office?" she asked.

"Good! Glad to have that job taken care of," Jack said, referring to his change in schedule. "Dad's pretty smart, you know. And he made me feel good about my contribution to solving the problem."

Ellen was pleased that Jack's response was mature and intelligent. Not at all belittling and arrogant, as she would have expected a year ago.

Then to her surprise, Jack asked, "Is there anything else you're wondering about?"

"No, just curious about how you're feeling in general with the accident and . . ."

"And the divorce," he finished the sentence for her.

"Yes, that too. I've felt as though I've been leaving you and Jenny out, so I guess I'm feeling a little guilty."

"No need to, Mom. I've never been the easiest kid to deal with. Never could keep my opinions to myself. I don't mean to be smug, but I know I often come off as a know-it-all."

Rather than saying something offensive, Ellen decided it best not to comment immediately. When she finally broke the silence, she said, "It's tough, isn't it? You just want someone to know what you think or how you feel, but then you end up hurting yourself even more."

"You got it, Mom. You hurt yourself because it hurts you to hurt someone else."

"I think you're right. Maybe we need to know how the other guy feels first. Then our words wouldn't sound so judgmental or out of place."

"Like talk less, listen more."

"That sounds like what my friend Anna would say. She might add that by listening we get to know each other." Then laughing, Ellen said, "Gosh, Jack, have we solved a lot of the world's problems!"

"Only if we learn to keep our mouths shut!"

"Or maybe swallow our own feelings when it benefits the situation, or we know more about the situation. Like you did when you shook hands with Al and thanked him for helping me."

"I thought you might have guessed that I resented Al. I wanted to be your extraordinary contractor, and I've been a little fearful that he could try to assume Dad's place in your life."

"Oh, Jack, I like Al a lot. He's easy to work with and has a lot of talent. You may have noticed that he has a handicap that he never allows to get in his way. But he's at least twenty years younger than me, and I'm not ready to be involved in another relationship. So put that thought out of your mind."

"Okay! If you say so." Seeing a Burgerville sign ahead, he added, "Hey, let's stop there and have some lunch."

Without having to acknowledge it, they both felt enough had been said. And what better way to leave one subject for another than to stop and eat. Jack drove into the parking lot and opened the door for his mother.

———

About two hours later, thanks to the GPS, they arrived at Anderson Tile and Stone. Jack had barely exited the car when a husky young man grabbed him from behind and let out a deep bellow. Jack reciprocated with a joyful shriek. Then the two bounced around, pounding each other's back.

Ellen sat in the car enjoying the antics of the two youthful friends, who obviously were excited to see each other. Then, without warning, they straightened up and seemed to become adults who had momentarily forgotten who they were. She thought it was like the music stopping in the middle of a crescendo. Watching them, she heard Jack mutter, "Come and meet my mother."

Stu appeared to be as eager to meet her as he was excited to see Jack. Reaching out to shake her hand, he said, "Graduation was so chaotic, I missed meeting you. Now here you are, and according to Jack, I might be able to help you out."

"That would be great, but in any case, I always enjoy meeting Jack's and Jenny's friends.

"Jack's been a good friend, and you know we have a lot in common. Not just WSU and the fraternity, but my grandfather, like Jack's was also an engineer, and you know how it goes in families. Once a Cougar, always a Cougar, plus now each of us works in our father's business."

"Goodness, that almost sounds like we should be related," Ellen remarked.

"Speaking of family, here comes my dad. He's been taking a customer around the stone yard."

"Hey, Dad! Jack and his mother are here."

Jim Anderson was as calm and self-contained as Stu was gregarious, and like Al, he was a get-to-the-point sort of person. Jack had met Stu's dad several times at father-son weekends in Pullman and was sure that his mother would get along well with him.

No sooner had they been introduced when Jim asked, "What can my business do to help with your summerhouse renovation?"

"I recently became aware of concrete countertops," Ellen said. "I think I'd like them in my new kitchen, but I haven't found a mason in the Land's End vicinity who would take on the job."

Here Jack jumped in. "I told Mom about Stu and how he had been working for you. Though a number of problems have to be addressed, maybe Stu or you could do the job."

"I was planning on taking some vacation time whenever Jack got here," Stu said. "Let's check our schedule and see how busy we are for the rest of the month."

"For the first time, I'm starting to feel hopeful," Ellen said. "We do need to talk about the cost, though, before I use up any more of your time. Where do you make the countertops? They would be awfully heavy to move, I would think."

"The cabinets have to be installed, and then we pour on site," Stu said.

"In that case, Jack, we need to check with Al to find out when they could be installed. "Jim, I'll call my contractor while you check your commitments and look over my floor plan."

They spent several hours making phone calls, calculating sizes, quantity, and cost of labor and materials. Jim talked a customer into delaying a small repair job. Al set a date for having the cabinets installed and ready for the countertops, and Stu scheduled his vacation time. Ellen offered to provide room and board for Stu while he poured and finished the counters. Jack volunteered to paint the cabinets and talked his dad into extending his vacation. Finally, their mission was accomplished, and Ellen took everyone out to dinner.

The next morning, Jim helped Ellen select floor tile for the renovation. They loaded the car with all the tile they had in stock and agreed that Stu would bring what they still needed from the new shipment when he drove to Land's End in about ten days.

Back on the road to Land's End, Ellen and Jack expressed their satisfaction in what they had accomplished—Ellen in getting her choice of counters and Jack in making his mother's wish a reality. After a while of relaxing in a state of euphoria, Jack said, "So, what's on your to-do list now?"

"After you've built your own home, you'll find it's never a done deal. You'll either add on or tear down or at least redecorate or repair something. In my case, I'll have to shop for furniture. You probably noticed that I only have the table and chairs in the dining area and your grandfather's big, old leather office chair. Which, by the way, I'm never going to get rid of."

"Well, if you do, I want it. It's the most comfortable chair I've ever sat in." Then he laughed. "Remember when I told you I wouldn't take a nap unless you let me sleep in grandfather's chair?"

"And then I didn't let him sit and read his paper until you woke up," Ellen recalled.

"How did he react to that?"

"I don't remember but he probably enjoyed the quiet. You were pretty noisy and demanding of his attention."

"Gosh, Mom, I really miss him. He was always very generous with his time—for me anyway."

The thought of David Holiday crossed her mind as she whispered, "He loved you a lot."

Ellen hadn't thought of David or Georgia for several days. Now with Jack having brought up the subject of her father, she wondered if she was ever going to find some peace of mind about them. And with the summerhouse feeling more like her home and Land's End becoming more familiar, she worried about running into them at the grocery store or The Bookstore.

"Dear God, help me handle that situation if it should ever occur," she said to herself.

Jack inserted a CD in the player, and they sat quietly listening until they reached the community where they had had lunch.

"Jack, want some lunch before we go any farther?"

"I could use a break. Besides, I've been wanting to tell you something."

"Important or interesting?"

"More on the interesting side, I think."

"Good. I'm more in the mood for interesting."

As soon as they had ordered, Ellen couldn't contain her curiosity any longer. "Okay, what's interesting? Have you fallen in love with someone I need to meet?"

"No, and neither has Dad."

"What!"

"I think Dad has changed his mind and might want to resume . . . his former relationship."

Ellen didn't respond. Not that a thousand things weren't racing through her head.

Finally, Jack blurted out, "With you, Mom! I think Dad might want to get back together with you. How would you feel about that?"

Caught off guard, Ellen murmured, "I don't know. I can't talk about it. Please understand, it's too personal." Getting up, she added, "Would you cancel my order? I'm sorry. I'm going outside. I need to move a bit."

Jack, too, left the table and canceled their lunch orders. He found his mother and silently walked with her until they found the car.

The silence continued until they reached Land's End. Before they arrived home, Jack made a quick stop at The Bookstore. He said, "You can wait in the car if you want, Mom. I'm just going to run in to pick up something Stu recommended by Desmond Tutu and the Dalai Lama. He thought I'd like it."

"Is it *Secret Joy*?" Ellen asked.

"Yes, have you read it?"

"I did. It's a good read."

After Jack's stop, neither said anything more. Al and his crew had finished work at the summerhouse for the day, so the house was as quiet as the car had been. Ellen grabbed her overnight bag and went straight to her room, got ready for bed, and spent much of the night talking to God.

———   ———

The next morning, Ellen woke up hearing her father's voice loud and clear. "One thing at a time, remember, one thing at a time."

"Okay," she said to her pillow.

#1. Renovation: all major decisions made.

#2. Jason: divorce—don't really know anything—only what Jack thinks.

#3. Georgia Holiday: she's the only one who can answer my questions. Call her! And so she did.

CHAPTER TEN

Before Ellen's parents left for Indiana last fall, they had the summerhouse interior painted. She wasn't sure what to call it. It wasn't white or cream or tan, but it had a minute drop of red that gave it a slight glow. She loved the hue. It made her feel warm, like having her mother nearby. And the tone would accept any accent color she might want to use.

With Stu arriving tomorrow, she decided that today was the day to do more furniture shopping. She needed to get new bedding for the queen bed that Al had helped her move from her parents' room to the guestroom for Stu. Buying furniture that would fill a whole room, let alone an entire house, was not Ellen's way of decorating. So, today she would just shop for bedding and two occasional chairs.

Jennifer Steel at Steel Furniture and Design had been a great help previously, so that was where Ellen headed with floor plan in hand.

Jennifer, who had a keen eye for decorating, said, "Ellen, why don't you check out these two warm-green leather swivel chairs. Will they meet your need?"

"I believe so," Ellen said. "I could place the chairs in the middle of the living room for a view of the fireplace or swing around on the other side of the room to watch TV. Or I could simply relax there after a hard day of renovating, I'll buy them but first I'll look for other decorating ideas."

Wandering around the store, Ellen nearly tripped over Georgia Holiday, who was sorting through a stack of throw pillows. Ellen quickly realized that the situation she had feared had just occurred.

"Ellen McCallister! Please excuse the mess I made. There are so many interesting designs: I'm having a hard time making up my mind," Georgia said.

"They're all very attractive," Ellen commented. "Maybe if you sorted by color, you could eliminate a few."

"That's a smart idea. My original thought had been to reflect the colors of our sunsets, which of course is in all of these. So, if I put the predominant red, orange, and gold colors in one pile and the purple, blue, and pink in another, it would reduce my distraction.

"That's right," Ellen said. "Then by eliminating unwanted sizes and shapes, you should have a manageable group to choose from. Good luck. By the way, do you still want to get together one of these days?"

"Of course. I'm sorry I haven't returned your call. We're here now. If you have the time, we could have coffee at Wanda's, or I live just a few blocks away. We could have some sun tea that I have in the fridge. We could visit there, and if I took a few of these pillows home, you could help me decide."

"That would be nice. However, my son's fraternity brother is arriving tomorrow, and I have to get the guestroom ready for him," Ellen said, holding up the bags of new bedding. "I can give you a call in a couple of days."

"That would be fine. I'm pretty free for the rest of the week, but Friday would be better than Saturday."

"I'll definitely keep that in mind," Ellen said as she continued on her way.

"Well, that wasn't so bad," she thought. "Why do I so often imagine and anticipate the worst? Georgia probably just wants to reminisce about some old time she and Dad had in college. No! That wasn't likely. More to the point, she probably just wants to get to know me better so she could anticipate any difficulty I might have with her son. On the other hand, she might not even know that I'm aware of my relationship to David. Feeling anxious but tired of the uncertainty, she said out loud, "Well, she'll know soon because I am going to call her and make arrangements for Friday."

——— ——

Friday morning nothing seemed to be going well. She dropped and broke her coffee cup and spilled coffee all over the dining room table. Worse than that, breakfast was a disaster. She burned the bacon, and her scrambled eggs turned out hard.

Fortunately, Jack and Stu laughed it off. "We had worse at the frat house, but I can't remember when," Jack said. While cleaning up (mostly throwing away paper plates and cups), Jack whispered, "Are you upset about something, Mom? You seem a bit anxious this morning."

"No, I just have to go into town this morning, and I would rather stay home and watch the cement pour. But, you know, you gotta do what you gotta do when you gotta do it." With that, she left the room to dress for meeting Georgia Holiday.

Before leaving, Ellen found Georgia's letter in her dad's desk and tucked it carefully in her jacket pocket, along with the newspaper clipping of David at the espresso stand at Driftwood Cove. She had decided that showing Georgia the letter would be the best way to present the subject she was most interested in learning about.

Arriving at the address Georgia had given her, Ellen estimated that the two-story weathered cedar shake house was about the same age as hers. The porch appeared to have recently been enclosed with windows. She admired the well-maintained yard and how the mature flowering shrubs, colorful perennials, and two beautiful shore pines framed the house. An S-curved walkway in which showy rocks, shells, and tile pieces had been strategically placed led to wide steps protected by an eyebrow overhang. It culminated in the most intriguing, but not ornate, carved door Ellen had ever seen. She was excited to see that the color of the window trim had been repeated on the trellis and doorlike gate to Georgia's very private front yard.

Ellen thought everything about the property attested to the work of very talented, deliberate artists. Even the hand-crafted brass doorbell she rang carried a cheerful, lyrical tune. Therefore, she was surprised when Georgia appeared with a shaved head, minimal makeup, no-nonsense black trousers, and the same faded green crewneck sweater she had worn the last two times Ellen saw her.

With a warm and cheerful smile, Georgia said, "Good morning, Ellen, so glad we could finally get together. Please come in. Can I get you some coffee, tea, or maybe some juice?"

"No, thank you—just finished breakfast, and I'm about coffeed out."

Georgia motioned her to a chair near the window. "Well, have a seat and tell me, how is the renovation going?"

"Very well. The concrete counters are being poured as we speak."

"This must mean you're nearly finished. How about painting?"

"Jack, my son, painted the new cabinet, and my parents had the entire interior painted before they left last fall, so it's just the addition that needs paint. Then the flooring, new appliances, and bathroom fixtures, and we'll be done."

"What about decorating and furniture?" Georgia inquired.

"Just a few new things for the living room, some barstools, and perhaps a new desk. I hate to get rid of Dad's old one, but it may be too large for the area I've dedicated for an office."

After an awkward pause, Ellen reached into her jacket pocket to retrieve Georgia's letter and said as casually as she could, "That reminds me. I found this letter when I was cleaning out his desk. I thought maybe we could talk about it."

Georgia took the letter but did not open it. After what seemed like forever to Ellen, Georgia said, "You knew nothing about this?"

"No."

"You must be wondering what kind of a woman you're talking to."

"Not really. I'm more in a quandary about how and when this came about and my father's response to it."

After a moment or two, Georgia said, "This may take a while." Getting up and going to her kitchen, she suddenly turned around. "Be assured! There is no doubt that John Underwood is David's father." She then left the room.

Ellen sat quietly. Looking around the room, she noticed that Georgia had selected pillows that perfectly suited the room and added to its warmth and charm. "This conversation has to be as hard for Georgia as it is for me," she thought.

As time passed, Ellen wondered, "Why aren't I feeling anxious about Georgia's long absence? Maybe it's because the room is filled with so many interesting distractions. Or maybe because I have to be here in order to find some peace regarding my father. On the other hand, maybe Georgia needs the time to face the question of her son's half sister. *Dear God, give us both your strength,*" she prayed.

The time finally came. Georgia returned carrying a carafe of coffee and a couple of cups. "Please excuse the delay. I thought we both might need some coffee by now."

Ellen accepted a cup and thanked her, not knowing where the conversation should go from there.

Georgia sat down on the chair next to Ellen. "I always knew this day, or one like it, would come when I would have to face my past eye to eye."

"I'm sorry I dumped this on you. My mind has been going in so many directions since I read that letter. And to be frank, I've mostly been concerned about how it affected me and my family. From the letter, I had to assume you're the only one who knew how all this came about and why the father I loved and who I thought loved me would leave me out of this part of his life and ignore another child he had. Who was he? Did Mother know?"

All the anxiety and uncertainty came flooding back, and she began to cry. Tears of anger, sadness, and confusion.

Georgia, who was shedding a few tears herself, reached out to Ellen with a handful of tissues. "I should start from the very beginning because, like you, I've mostly thought of how this story affected me, a pretty, young black woman. A lot of people at that time thought women like me used sex to get a husband or anything else they might want."

"I never thought of you that way," Ellen assured her. "I really didn't. Please believe me!"

"Times have changed, but there is still a large population that holds that opinion. Thank you for not being one of them. Because of what you said, I think it would be good for both of us if I tell the whole story. The John Underwood I knew and perhaps didn't know.

"My parents moved from the South to Portland during the Second World War and then, with a lot of African Americans, moved on to Seattle, where my aunt Jane and uncle Benjamin already lived. Work was plentiful. My father was a carpenter and mother a schoolteacher. They did very well. Blacks were accepted, not totally, but certainly better than in most of the South. Seattle was a good environment, especially for an inquisitive little girl who loved going to school.

"One summer we took a rare long weekend trip and discovered the community of Land's End.

"Both my parents liked the idea of being out of the city, as did a growing population that wanted small cottages for weekend retreats and summer vacations. Of course, with that growing population came stores and other businesses and eventually schools. So, Land's End became the place I called home. My father built houses, and my mother taught primary classes in school.

"My parents believed that education was the only way to equalize and make the races acceptable to each other. There was no doubt in their minds that I was going to get a college education. That was just fine by me. I loved learning new things, but I didn't know which course of study would lead to a profitable and

78

accessible occupation. In high school, my strongest subjects were in mathematics. My geometry teacher encouraged me to consider engineering.

In those days it was considered more a male profession, but my parents thought if a boy could do it, a girl could do it, too. And why not their daughter? I don't know if they knew the relationship in numbers between black and white students at the university. But it wouldn't have mattered if they did. The same thing would have applied to the relationship of male students to female students in engineering. If I was the only girl, well, I would just have to work harder. Turned out I loved it and did very well.

"I lived with Aunt Jane and Uncle Benjamin in Seattle and would go home to Land's End as often as possible, so consequently socializing on campus was minimal, even if I wasn't black. Plus, I learned quickly to ignore the off-color remarks directed my way from white male classmates, except not from your father, who was always a very civil gentleman. Perhaps partly because we saw each other a few times when he was visiting your grandparents in Land's End.

"Engineering, like most fields of study, has a couple of brain buster subjects. For John and me, it was analytical geometry. Our instructor suggested we have a study partner and commit to working together on a regular basis so that we would never get behind and would be constantly reviewing. The men in the class quickly got their partners, and to my surprise, John approached me and said, 'I see no one picked the smartest student in the class. Want to help me out?'

"After that, we worked twice a week wherever we could find a quiet place. When the semester was coming to an end, anxiety doubled around final exams. No one, including John and me, could handle the thought of failing and having to repeat the class the next semester. But finding a place to study was getting almost impossible. Knowing that I lived in Land's End, he suggested we study the weekend before the final at his parents' cottage in Land's End. He said he was sure his mom had left some canned soup and stuff we could eat.

"My parents were concerned about the plan but knew John's parents and how important it was that we do well on the finals. After much discussion, they agreed not to stand in our way. We started at eight o'clock on Saturday morning and continued until eight that night. Sunday morning my parents dropped me off again on their way to church. Late afternoon, I told John I had to rest. I remember my eyes burning and having a miserable headache. John got me a couple of aspirins from the kitchen cupboard and suggested I lie down in the downstairs bedroom.

"I woke several hours later and saw John lying beside me. He asked how I was feeling. I muttered 'better' and turned over and fell back to sleep. When I awoke again, he was lying against me with his arm around me. I imagine you can guess the rest.

"The test was grueling hard. But our studying paid off because we both did very well. Neither of us spoke of the situation. John left for Indiana at the end of the semester, and I got a summer job at a local coffee and sandwich shop to help with the next year's expenses. Just prior to the new semester, I realized I was pregnant. My parents were more than a little disappointed in me. They were ashamed! They arranged with my aunt and uncle in Seattle for me to live with them. They didn't have any children, and when David was born, they fell in love with him and wanted us to stay. About two years later, I went back and got my degree. Aunt Jane and Uncle Benjamin helped me raise him until I married my husband, who has been a wonderful father."

Engrossed in the story, Ellen envisioned Georgia as a young single mother. Suddenly, she blurted out, "What happened to Dad? Surely he couldn't have abandoned you—not you and the baby!"

"I never talked to him until a few years ago. You have to realize, Ellen, your father and I were study partners, not lovers! He never knew that I became pregnant. As a young black woman who shamed her parents and herself at that time in history, it didn't occur to me to let him know, and I believed Aunt Jane when she said he probably wouldn't have believed me."

"So, what happened then—a few years ago? Wasn't it awkward to run into him on the street or in a store?"

"That rarely happened, but when it did, I usually turned and walked away."

"I can understand that," Ellen said. "When we were on vacation here, if Dad wasn't on the golf course, he was usually in his office keeping up with work from home.

"How did you decide to tell him? He was a retired man. Why, David must have been nearly retired, too. How old is he? Anyway, he certainly didn't need another father anymore."

"I don't know, Ellen. I guess I just couldn't keep it to myself anymore. Or maybe the story just had to have an ending."

"Until now. Now there's me. I'm sort of a sister with children. I've added another chapter now. Where does the story really end? Do family secrets stay secrets? Should they?"

"I don't know the answer to that either, but God knows, I've had years to think about it. But right now, I do feel better for the telling of my part anyway. If I told David about a sister and that she lives here in Land's End, would he want to meet you? How would you feel about that?"

"Someday I'd probably like that. But right now, I have to get a few other things in my life straightened out. I'm feeling better about my father, though. Thank you for telling me your side of the situation. I know it couldn't have been easy."

"You're welcome. Thank you for listening and not judging." Georgia stood up and put her arms out to embrace Ellen. "I'd get your permission before I ever said a word. By the way, did my blackness have anything to do with your feelings?"

"No, goodness no!" She reached out to accept Georgia's hug. "Except I've never met a beautiful woman brave enough to shave her head."

Both women laughed in relief as Georgia walked Ellen to the door.

Ellen drove away feeling a sense of calm that she hadn't experienced for a long time. She whispered, as she always did, "*Thank you.*" Moments later, her cellphone rang. It was Jack. "Hi, Mom, are you still in town?"

"I am. Something you need before I come home?"

"I'm going to run out of varnish before I finish the second coat on the window trim. If you can pick up a quart, I can finish before dinner."

"Great. See you soon, I'm having lunch with a friend, then picking up a roasted chicken for dinner tonight."

"And mashed potatoes?" Jack asked.

"And asparagus!"

"Sounds good. See you soon, Mom."

On her way to meet George at Wanda's, Ellen stopped to buy the varnish. There she ran into Anna so invited her to join them for lunch. The three of them had become close friends, but with all the work on the house, Ellen had not seen either one for a couple of weeks. Now they had time to enjoy catching up on their lives: George's recent sale of a cottage at Harbor Shores, Anna's vegetable garden that was producing more than she could eat.

Of course, Ellen was eager to tell about Jack and Stu's visit and their work on the remodel. "By the time I get home, Stu will have poured the concrete for the countertops," she said. And with a quick wink at Anna, she added, "I had coffee with Georgia Holiday before coming here for lunch."

"Be careful with that one," George said. "Before you know it, she'll have you working on every committee in Land's End that she heads up."

"Well, that might not be bad since it looks like I'll be living here at least for a year or two. I'll need something to do."

"Why just a year or two?" George asked.

With no explicit reason intended, Ellen replied, "I'm sure you've heard how children and especially grandchildren can pull you in their direction."

"That reminds me," George said, "I need to show a house to a young, growing family that will be moving to Land's End. See you ladies soon, I hope."

With George gone, Anna asked, "How did your morning with Georgia go?"

"It all went well," Ellen assured her. "I'm feeling much better about my father's part with regard to David. As you might expect, our meeting was not easy for Georgia either, but she was glad we had met and had time to talk. After I have more time to mull it over, I hope we can have a good long visit."

"I'm relieved to hear that you are feeling more at peace, Ellen."

Jack and Stu had peeled the potatoes and set the dining room table by the time Ellen arrived with the varnish, chicken, and asparagus. "Mom, look what we accomplished while you were away!"

Ellen was thrilled with the long-awaited concrete countertops and gave both young men a grateful hug for their part in getting them. "Let's all toast this accomplishment with a glass of wine, and then I'll finish preparing dinner," she said.

"I'll second that," said Jack. "After I finish that last bit of varnishing, our work will be done. By the way, Stu and I are going to the beach tomorrow. Al wants us out of the house so the tile can be laid in the addition."

CHAPTER ELEVEN

Jack and Stu had enjoyed their day off at Driftwood Cove so much that they decided to go back since all the work on the renovation was completed—at least all that they could do. They both had a few days' vacation left to hike, surf, or just hang around and get to know Brenda Holiday, the espresso and sandwich proprietor. She and Stu had already exchanged phone numbers and made tentative plans to meet again.

By the time they got back to Land's End, Ellen had a good start on making the summerhouse into the Ellen McCallister home. She loved the natural light and being able to see through to windows in the addition and out to the garden. She arranged dishes on the open shelves and designated a place in the walk-in pantry for anything that didn't have to be in the kitchen. Al had left an opening in the kitchen bar to put a cart John had built for Mary, the idea being to save steps in taking items to and from the pantry.

Everything was working out well, but what she liked best was the 18-inch-wide stack of shelves just to the left of the sink for a coffee bar. The placement was handy to the dining room as well as the kitchen bar and water for the Keurig coffeemaker. The top shelf allowed for hanging a variety of different wine glasses.

She had made a few more purchases at Steel Furniture and Design. A desk with cabinets above it for office supplies helped separate Ellen's office area from the living room. And just because she liked it, she bought a little bistro set that fit perfectly against the wall between the kitchen and addition. She could imagine sitting there having a beverage with Anna. In the winter, it might add a spot of color in that area.

Still on order were two matching chesterfields that would face each other in front of the fireplace. They were upholstered in a linen and polyester fabric that appeared to be hand painted with colors of branches, leaves, and a scattering of red berries. She had heard that a room wasn't complete until it included a little red. True or not, she thought it added to the warmth of the room.

At this point, Ellen wanted to quit thinking about the summerhouse. Jack would be leaving soon, and she needed to know how it would feel to live there alone. Had she really made a new home for herself? There were a few things in Indiana that she wanted. She hoped that she could keep the list simple and short so that she would feel free to ask Jenny to arrange for shipping. As of now, the last thing she wanted to do was go back to Indiana and start dismantling the place she used to call "home!" Knowing that she would not be living there, she had already packed her books, a favorite lamp, and a couple of pictures from her parents' home.

The thought had also occurred to her that it would take more than a house to make Land's End home. George had suggested (satirically, Ellen thought) that Georgia could take care of that. In Indiana she had been involved in a couple of volunteer and group activities at her church. She helped with the church news-letter once a month and every Tuesday made sack lunches for the homeless. She enjoyed meeting with both groups but quickly realized that in Land's End, a few volunteer jobs would still leave a lot of empty hours to fill the void left by the absence of family. "Maybe I should get a job," she thought, "but after the estate is settled and probably the divorce, too."

Deep in thought, she picked up her phone and said, "Hello" before check-ing to see who was calling.

"Hi, Ellen. Jason here. You got a minute?"

"Of course. What's up? Jenny and family okay?"

"They're fine. I just had lunch with Jenny. She told me about the summer-house makeover and that you were hoping to get Shazey soon."

"I have been missing him. I'm sure she told you I'll be staying here for some time."

"Well, Jack's coming home tomorrow, and I'm going to have some free time in a few weeks. We really should talk, and I'd like to see what you've been doing to the house."

"Slow down, Jason! Are you saying you want to come to Land's End and bring Shazey?"

"In a word, yes!" Then, almost inaudibly, he added, "How would you feel about that?"

"I agree there are things we should talk about," she managed to say. "I'm sure Shazey would be much happier riding with you than crammed in a crate on a plane. Or maybe you weren't planning on driving?"

"No. I think a road trip would be good for me right now. Jenny mentioned that you wanted some more clothes that she had packed. I could bring them at the same time unless you need them sooner. In that case, Jenny or I could mail them."

Ellen smiled. It was good to hear his voice. She remembered how much more she learned from the sound of his voice than from his actual words. The faster he talked, the more uncertain he was. The more fearful of a response, the quieter he became. The more resolute he was, the bolder his voice grew.

"No, I don't need them right now. A few more weeks will be fine. You may recall that it's sweatshirt weather here all the time, so my one pair of dress slacks, white blouse, and blazer are acceptable for church or lunch with a friend. I'll have time to refresh the upstairs after Jack and Stu leave tomorrow."

"Great!" he said with a loud emphasis on the "t." "I'll let you know my schedule soon." Here Ellen noticed that his voice was soft but his speech rapid.

"Hmm. What was behind that," she wondered as she hung up the phone. Then she thought that maybe he was questioning his motives and feelings about making a big change in his life. Like she felt about The Bookstore, she loved the new style but missed the comfortable, familiar old room.

While Ellen was pondering her conversation with Jason, Jack and Stu came downstairs. Stu, with his suitcase in hand, said, "I'll be heading home this afternoon. Thank you for giving me some time to spend with Jack."

Ellen gave him a warm hug. "Come back whenever you can—or whenever you're on your way to Driftwood Cove."

When Stu left, Jack said, "Since this is my last night on the coast, how about I take you to the Oyster Shack for dinner?"

"Great! We both love oysters, and we don't have to shower and change to go there and have the best oysters on the coast. What time do you want to leave?"

"Oh, I don't know. Is five thirty or six o'clock, okay?"

"Sounds fine. I'd like to finish unpacking this box for the pantry, and maybe you would like to try out the new washer and dryer. That way you could go home with a suitcase full of clean clothes."

"Super idea," Jack said as he started upstairs.

"Al is in the garage finishing some shelves for Grandmother's armoire that I'm going to put at the dining room end of the addition. Maybe he would like to go with us."

"Mom, you know I do like Al, but this is my last evening here. Let's not. We haven't had much time alone since I came and practically none since we got home from Anderson Tile and Stone."

Realizing how little time they had actually had, she replied, "Good thought. It will just be a mother-son date."

On the way to the pantry, she turned to watch him go up the stairs two at a time.

"My son has become quite a young man," she thought. "A year ago, I would not have looked forward to spending an evening alone with him."

The Oyster Shack was a family favorite but mostly a place she and Jason had enjoyed as a getting away when Jenny and Jack were teenagers. It literally was a shack. When customers walked in, the door slammed behind them, and they grabbed a number from a stack hanging on the wall. They handed it to a waiter and told him how many oysters they wanted. Then they wandered over to a stainless trough where earlier the shuckers had stood shelling and washing the oysters that had just been dropped off.

At five o'clock, the trough became an old-fashioned salad bar—the kind with peas, sliced beets, and chopped-up hard-boiled eggs and containers of Kraft Catalina and Italian dressing.

After finding a table, customers ate their salads. Soon the waiter in jeans and a sweatshirt brought the oysters and took the drink (beer) orders. Delish! Ellen could hardly wait to go.

A loud buzz signaled that Jack's clothes were ready for the dryer. She reminded Jack, "Take a sweater or jacket because it's always cool at the Shack."

All the way there, Ellen and Jack reminisced about funny family stories, and they discussed oysters: different ways they liked oysters (fried, stewed, on the half shell), the size they liked best, their favorite oyster dips, who made the best ones, and so on.

"This was a marvelous idea. Can't believe this is my first time going to the Shack since arriving this spring," Ellen said.

"And I can't believe I'm going back to Indiana in the morning and missed a trip or two while I've been here, I didn't even get Stu out here. You'll have to make sure he gets a Shack experience when he comes through. He'd love it."

"Do you really think oysters would slow him down on his way to Driftwood Cove to see a certain young lady?

"Probably not, but I bet he'd stop on his way back." Jack laughed at the thought.

"Well, here we are," Ellen said as they pulled into a parking spot. "Have you decided how many you'll order?"

"I'm up for a nice round dozen, and you?"

"Eight one-or-two biters. My usual order," Ellen replied.

When the oysters arrived at their table, Jack wondered, "Do you know anyone else who orders these oysters by the number of bites in each one?"

"It was Mrs. Chin, the long-time owner of the Shack, who explained that children can better understand the size of a bite they put in their mouth as opposed to something small, medium, or large. I imagine she taught quite a few children to order their oyster dinners that way. Then your dad taught you that the size indicated how you liked your oysters, but the number determined how hungry you were," Ellen said.

"Gosh, Mom, was there anything you and Dad didn't have to teach me? My favorite memory was being allowed to order my own dinner. I remember when the server said, 'And what will this little man have?' I thought he was being condescending, but I sat up straight, looked right at him, and said, 'I'll have half a dozen of your one biters, please.'

"You and Dad knew I was trying to irritate him. But I always wanted to do everything the way Dad did. Would you have corrected me if I'd ordered a full dozen?"

"Probably not. Your dad usually felt that experience was a better teacher than a correction. Anyway, what I remember about that dinner is that we all went home full and happy!"

"I can hardly wait to tell Dad what I did my last night in Land's End."

"I'm sure he'll be glad to hear and probably a bit envious. He loves the Shack."

"You haven't mentioned him since we left Anderson's. Care to talk about how you're feeling now?"

"No, actually I haven't given it a lot of thought. Maybe if he brings it up, I'll have a better sense of how I feel."

"Is Dad coming here—to Land's End? To see you?"

"In a couple of weeks, he's bringing Shazey."

"Well, I'll be!"

"Yeah, me too."

— ⚊

Ellen stopped at Anna's to relax and visit for a while after she dropped Jack off at the airport. She wanted to talk to a woman about something other than renovating an old summerhouse.

"Jason called and said he's planning to come to Land's End and bring Shazey."

"How do you feel about that?" Anna asked.

"Like I told Jack, I honestly don't know. It would be interesting to hear what he has to say. All I really know is what Jack thought. Maybe Jason just needs a short vacation from work, and bringing Shazey will give him a destination."

"Are you going to let him stay at the house?"

"Yes, there are two guestrooms upstairs. I'm sure he won't be staying any longer than he feels he has to. Maybe a couple of days. Whatever the case, we do have a lot to discuss."

"Like a reconciliation?" Anna asked.

"I'm not saying that could never happen, but I'm certainly not ready for anything like that now." On a lighter note, she added, "Besides, I need to experience living alone in my newly remodeled house. My home . . . alone."

"Good thinking."

Ellen also wanted to set a time for Anna and George to see all that she had accomplished and to have lunch. She and Anna decided Saturday would be best if George was available. "Maybe Al could to come, too," Ellen said.

She left Anna's with a plan to stop at George's office and then go to the market. She had already made her list for making quiche, a simple green salad, and fresh peaches for dessert.

George saw her coming and left his desk to meet her at the door. "You and Al must be winding up the renovation. I've seen you twice already this month."

"Yes, it's partially decorated, which is why I'm here. Anna's coming for lunch on Saturday, and I'm hoping you, if you're not too busy, and Al can join us. I'm in the mood to do some showing off."

"I'll check my calendar. No. For lunch and to see the house, I'll clear my calendar and make new arrangements if need be."

"Good. About noon or twelve thirty. See you," and she was off to the market.

After cooking for Jack and Stu and sometimes Al for the past several weeks, Ellen had become quite familiar with the store layout. This made finding items on her list faster, and it made her feel more like Land's End was home.

First Ellen bought all the ingredients for the quiche lorraine as well as paper napkins and Fruit-Fresh to keep the peaches from turning brown. Then she headed for the produce department to find peaches that were ripe or nearly ripe. With only two grocery stores in Land's End, Ellen wasn't surprised to see Georgia Holiday sorting through the bin of peaches.

"Hello, Ellen," Georgia said. She appeared distracted.

"Good to see you, Georgia. I want some peaches too, but I'm not familiar with West Coast varieties. What do you recommend?"

"These veterans are quite good. I've found nearly enough for our dessert tonight."

While they continued sorting and visiting, Ellen heard a man's voice. "Mom, what about these?"

Without looking up, Georgia said, "Oh, Ellen, this is my son, David Holiday."

Caught off guard, Ellen laid the peach she was holding back in the pile while Georgia told David, "Ellen McCallister is a new resident of Land's End."

Ellen turned to greet him. Hoping not to stare, she held out her hand. "Good to meet you, Mr. Holiday."

"Nice to meet you, too. Most people just call me David."

"And I'm Ellen. Who's fixing the peaches tonight?" she asked in an effort to make light conversation.

"In case you're wondering about my grubby sweatshirt and jeans, I'm going to grill the fish my dad and I caught today, but Mom's better in the dessert department. Her peach pie is the best. It's my daughter Brenda's favorite."

"We're celebrating her birthday tonight," Georgia explained.

"My son, Jack, and his fraternity brother met her when they spent some time at Driftwood Cove this past week."

"I met him and his friend briefly when I stopped to see Brenda. Nice young men.

At that point, Georgia interrupted. "David, we'd better be going if I'm to have this pie done before the girls get there!" Turning to Ellen, she said, "I'll be talking to you soon."

"Okay," David replied. "If you've found enough peaches, let's go. Nice to meet you, Ellen. Maybe I'll see you sometime at my mother's."

Ellen watched as they walked away, wondering if there was anything about him that resembled her father. He was about the same height, and he folded his arms across his chest the same way her father had when he listened to her. But other than that, she didn't see any similarities. She tried to dismiss the situation by continuing to select peaches but couldn't seem to let it go. She knew it was inevitable that someday they would meet, and all things considered, this encounter had thankfully gone quite well.

When Ellen got home, she was surprised to see Al's truck. "Hi, glad to see you. Are you measuring for the window boxes Mr. Green Jeans suggested?"

"Yes, I was driving by and thought if I had your drawing and the measurements, the crew could put them together next week. Should I get one of the guys to paint them, too?"

"No, I have plenty of time and can do it. I was going to call you. Anna and George are coming to see the house and have lunch on Saturday, and I'd like to have you come, too, if you have the time. Besides, you should be there to hear all the oohs and aahs they will express."

"Yeah, always good to hear your work is appreciated. Can I come in my work clothes? What time?"

"Of course. Will noon or twelve thirty work for you?"

"Sure, Thanks for the invite, Ellen." Then he drove away.

— —

When Anna and George arrived, Ellen explained the reasoning behind all the changes and the addition to the back of the house that gave her access to the bathroom, laundry, and storage plus a view of her mother's garden.

"The chesterfields arrived a few days early, so the living room is readier for company," she said. "It's by no means decorated, but it certainly looks more inviting."

Anna and George both remarked that they were impressed with the changes. George, of course, saw it from the standpoint of how much value was added.

Being practical, Anna focused on Ellen's frugal but adequate use of space in the kitchen and pantry. As a devoted dog person, Anna said, "I love the area under the stairs for Shazey's bed."

Al soon joined them. They all expressed their enthusiasm for the addition and complimented him on the attractiveness of the cabinet.

"It was my idea," Al said, "but kudos go to Ellen. She was the one who designed the practical features to fit her needs."

Ellen then served the lunch. Her friends agreed that the menu was very delicious. The men boasted about being real men, even if they really enjoyed the quiche lorraine. Sliced ripe peaches and Anna's homemade sugar cookies quickly disappeared. All three were grateful for her tasty contribution to their lunch.

"Could I take one more?" George asked. "I have to leave to finish a listing."

Following suit, Al grabbed another cookie as he left the table, "If George can have another, so can I. I have to meet a new customer in about twenty minutes."

To which Ellen shook her head. Pretending to mock them, she said, "Go! Go! Anna and I don't have to go to work. I think we'll just have some girl talk and another cookie—if there are any left," she said, looking at an empty plate. Ellen went to say good-bye to George and Al. Then to Anna, she said, "Come and try out the new couches with me. See if I made a good decision. I'll bring us more coffee."

Anna was not comfortable asking personal questions, but on this occasion, she was anxious to know how her friend was handling yet another surprise. So, she calmly inquired, "Care to talk about that call from Jason?"

"That and David, who I met a day ago," Ellen replied.

"Really? And how did that come about?"

"That's what I love about you. You always seem to know when I need to talk. And I feel safe expressing my feelings with you. Thanks for asking."

"So, which one do you want to get off your mind first?"

"There's not much to tell about Jason. When you asked if I was going to let him stay at the house, without thinking, I said yes. Now I realize that may not be a good idea. First, I'd be preparing dinner, then breakfast. Then soon he'd be telling me what he wanted for lunch, and before I knew it, out of habit, I'd be doing all the things I used to do, and we wouldn't have solved any of the problems that brought us to our separation."

"I think you're right," Anna said. "Have you thought how you'll handle it?"

"When he calls with his schedule, I think I'll invite him over for dinner and ask if he wants me to make hotel reservations for him nearby."

"That's a good plan—cordial but not overly hospitable or intimate. What if Jack was right, and he wants to reestablish the marriage?"

"There are so many things we need to discuss before that—like Sonja. Money. The children. Trust!

"Clearly, you've been giving his visit a lot of serious and reasonable thought."

"I always believed Jason and I had a strong relationship, so I was very shocked when he told me about Sonja and that he wanted a divorce.

"It's not the plan I had for my life, but Jason's a pretty reasonable person. It may be very awkward at first. But I'm sure we can work it out. I feel resigned to that."

Anna seemed to know exactly when enough had been said, and she didn't push for more. Instead, she complimented her on her rational and generous thinking. "You always try to put the best construction on everything."

"You may be giving me too much credit. He did hurt me a lot, and I can get angry and mouthy."

"So, you're normal. So what!" Anna said in an effort to dismiss the subject. "What about David? Was that meeting planned, or did it just sneak up on you?"

"As you might expect, I stopped to pick up what I needed for today's lunch and saw Georgia. It didn't register that the other person picking out peaches might be David until he responded to our conversation, and Georgia introduced him. It was clear he had no idea who I was, so we just engaged in some small talk about peaches and what they were doing that night until Georgia said they needed to be going. He said perhaps he would see me again at his mother's house."

"Any impressions that stood out?"

"He was certainly pleasant enough. He was about the same height as my dad, and he crossed his arms on his chest the way my dad did when he listened to me. Nothing else made me think, 'yes, you are my father's son.' Georgia called me this morning to assure me that she had not disclosed anything about me. She just wanted to know that I wasn't worried. She's a very lovely person."

"That has to make things easier for you."

"Yes, it does. I don't have to worry about what she might or might not say or when she would say it. I've decided that I'll probably tell Jason about David, so he can weigh in on sharing the information with Jenny and Jack."

"Probably a good idea. What affects you and Jason is bound to elicit some response from your children. Jason is their father, of course," Anna said.

"And David is their uncle. Oh, Anna, sometimes I think it would be easier to just tell the whole story and let the chips fall where they may. That couldn't be worse than lying awake at night worrying about a lot of ifs. Like what if it was Jack rather than Stu who was infatuated with Brenda Holiday, and he ended up wanting to marry his cousin and then was heartbroken and angry with me about keeping his grandfather's secret?"

Out of concern for her friend, Anna whispered, "I suppose that could happen, but aren't we borrowing trouble?"

"Could be but saying it out loud always seems to help me. And I can always add, '*Please, God,*' when I'm talking to him. Besides, I'm sure no problem is going to be solved by drinking coffee and eating cookies."

Standing up, Anna said, "Then let's get up and clean up our lunch mess."

CHAPTER TWELVE

Ellen had just reached the top of the stairs with an armload of fresh bed linen and towels when the home phone rang, but she couldn't answer in time. "I need to get a phone for up here or carry a charged cell with me at all times," she thought.

Since she needed a hammer and hook to hang a mirror, she decided to get them right away and bring the phone upstairs. The call was from Al. His message said that he was on his way over with a brilliant idea.

"Well, that's exciting," she said to herself, as she gathered up all the items she needed in a basket and set it on one of the steps to take upstairs. Then she made sure there was enough water in the Keurig, fixed a couple of cups of coffee, and brought out the last two cookies Anna had hidden in the kitchen on Saturday. Just then Al arrived at the back door.

"Good morning, Al. I'm eager to hear about the brainstorm you had last night."

"A good thought, anyway, I hope. Thanks for the coffee and cookie."

"Have a seat and please tell me about your idea."

"You may recall when I left on Saturday—great lunch by the way—I mentioned that I had a meeting with a new client. Well, I did. Nice young couple. They closed on a lot right in town, selected a house plan, and were prequalified. They knew what kind of a time schedule they were looking at." With a sigh, he said, "That's where their agreement ended. For the rest of the afternoon, she told me what she had to have, and he told me what they didn't need. Unfortunately, the two lists were nearly the same."

"Hmm, that had to be confusing, even embarrassing. How did you handle it?"

"First of all, this was extreme but not entirely unusual. I finally took their plan and all my notes and said I would do my best and get back to them the first of the week.

"After mulling it all over the rest of the day, I came up short. Nothing satisfied me. I left the office and went to the shop to do something physical, like sand flower boxes. By nine o'clock, I was tired so went home, showered, and went to bed. On Sunday morning, I woke with my brilliant idea."

"Well, don't keep me waiting. What did you come up with? And why are you telling me all this?"

"Because my last client—you—are the answer!"

"Me? How? Al, you've been working too hard or need more coffee."

"Yes, you, Ellen McCallister, can solve this problem for me. Remember when you first talked to me about renovating the summerhouse? You said that for it to become your home, it had to have specific storage, a place for everything and everything in its place. That's what would make a house feel like your home."

"Okay, I did say that. How does that help you?"

"You! Yes, you become part of my crew! When I get a new customer, get their house plan, budget, and time schedule, I'll tell them that part of my fee would include their talking to you about how they see themselves living in their new house.

"You would learn about their particular interests, hobbies, collections, pets. Do they like to entertain? Do they have children? What do their children like to do if it's raining and they can't go outside? Is anyone in the family a musician, artist, athlete? Are they outdoor people? Fishing, hunting, skiing, golf? All these things take room, and if they're passionate about them, it becomes frustrating if they don't have the space to practice, enjoy, or store equipment.

"Can you see how this kind of information would save me time and help me produce a building that wouldn't just be a house but would be their home?" he asked.

"Yes, I can. It's a wonderful plan, and I know you would have very satisfied, happy clients. I just am not sure I'm up for the job."

"Ellen, I know you can! Because you did! Take yourself back to the days you were trying to figure out what you would need to not just update the summer-house but also make it your home or a saleable vacation home for a buyer.

"Your struggle was not about what you needed based on your likes and dislikes. It was in finding the place to work, play, and entertain. And you didn't want to spend half your day looking for all the things you needed to accomplish the project and the storage adequate for the task."

"And I wanted it to look nice without spending all my money," Ellen added.

"Exactly!"

"It would be fun meeting and getting to know new residents, and this would certainly not be a full-time job."

"Right."

"And I wouldn't be making any decisions for them. We would just be talking about how they would see living in their new house."

"That's it. You would basically guide them in making decisions for themselves. I'm the one who would have to figure out how to accomplish it. Like where to put six bicycles for six kids when not in use, a gourmet kitchen for the family chef, a grand piano for the young musician, the TV room, storage for books and board games and skis and golf clubs plus gardening tools, and two big cars—everything in a 2,400-square-foot house. And, oh yes, room for the family Newfoundland canine member."

Laughing until tears were running down her face, Ellen said, "I can't say yes, but I will say that I'll give it a lot of thought."

"I can't ask for anything more than that," Al replied. "After working with you, I'm sure you'll do a great job, so I hope you'll agree. You have more sisu than you realize. I can't think of anyone I would trust with this idea more than you."

"Thank you for the reassurance, Al. I really will give it serious thought. Can I have a couple of days?"

"For sure!" Then getting up to leave, he said, "Just don't sell yourself short."

After walking Al to the door, Ellen picked up the basket with the phone and other items to take upstairs. She still needed to finish cleaning the bathroom, put clean sheets on the beds, and hang the mirror, but good intentions were as far as she got. Her dad's old office chair, which Jack had moved upstairs, beckoned her to sit and think about the job. "You never know when you wake up in the morning what God has planned for you," she thought.

After a couple of days talking to God, Ellen told Al that she would try interviewing a new customer about his or her conception of life in a new house. "There's nothing to lose," she concluded. "If it ends up that neither of us is satisfied with the outcome, I can just stack it up to an interesting experience. And you did say you rarely had more than one house going at a time, so I won't be confining myself to a grueling schedule. Maybe a half day to interview and another day writing up a report."

"I doubt that it would be less, but every situation will be different. So, there could be cases that would take a little more time," Al said. "And by the way, what kind of recompense could make you say yes?"

"I think I'll ask George what he pays his office manager and then calculate an hourly rate."

"That's a good idea. Why don't you do that, let me know, and we can talk again soon."

They shook hands on it, and Ellen said, "Right now I have to get ready for company in a few days."

"Showing off the house again?

"Yes and no. Jason is bringing Shazey, my dog, and wants to see what I've done to the summerhouse,"

"Oh, oh, is that going to be a problem?"

"No, as far as I know, he just needed some time away from the office and was interested in seeing the house. Jack probably told him some of the things we did. Remember, I told you he is an architect so is naturally interested. Besides, we have some financial things to discuss. Then, as if she suddenly remembered, she added, "And divorce."

— ⬩ ⬩ —

The remainder of the week after Al offered her a job, Ellen spent working on the house to make it look more like her home than a residence ready to put on the market. She had saved a small table from the estate sale and put it between the swivel chairs. She bought a set of everyday dishes and water and wine glasses to put on the open shelves. But she left room for pieces she might accumulate or retrieve from the Indiana house, such as the watermelon salad bowl Jenny had painted for them. It reminded her to put it on the list of things to talk to Jason about. By Sunday there was not much left to do except make the pasta shrimp salad that would keep until Jason arrived.

By midafternoon, Jason arrived almost exactly at the time he planned. Ellen watched at the kitchen sink as he drove up, and then she went to the back door to meet him and Shazey. Jason came carrying a large bouquet of mixed flowers.

"Hi, how was the trip?" As Jason extended the bouquet, she said, "What's with the flowers?"

"Hi, yourself. I thought a guest always brought the hostess a gift. Not knowing your color scheme, I thought a mixed variety would work. Trip was fine. No problems."

"Well, thank you, but certainly not necessary. Shazey would be gift enough." Looking around, she said, "Where is he now? Shazey, here boy!"

Turning away from her, he said louder than the situation called for, "Ellen, stop! He couldn't make it."

"Jason, where is he? What do you mean he couldn't make it?" Now Ellen felt anxious and worried.

"Can't we go inside? I'll tell you."

"Yes, of course. You just left him home? Is Jenny taking care of him? How could you make a decision like that without telling me? I'm so disappointed. I was really looking forward to having him here with me."

"Stop, Ellen!" Then more quietly, he said, "Let's sit down, and I'll tell you what happened."

Knowing she would not learn anything until she stopped talking, Ellen willed herself to be still.

Jason sat in one of the swivel chairs and turned to see her. Slowly but distinctly and quietly, he began, "Shazey had been acting strangely, eating a bare minimum. You know how he liked his meals. But no matter how much I coaxed him, he just seemed to mope around and rub his jaw on the carpet, never jumping up and laying his head on my lap like he always did when I watched the evening news. I finally called Clark. He said to bring him to the clinic, which of course, I did. Turned out he had a huge abscess. Clark put him on antibiotics, and . . ." Jason nearly cried. "He didn't make it through the surgery."

"I'm sorry, Ellen. I know you were looking forward to seeing him and how much we both loved the little piss ant" (the favorite name for him when he misbehaved).

Ellen went to the kitchen and poured herself a glass of water and then handed a glass to Jason.

"Thank you, but I think I'll have a glass of wine, if you don't mind."

"Help yourself. There's a corkscrew left of the sink."

Returning to the couch, Ellen asked, "So, what did Dr. Clarkson say was the reason?"

"He said Shazey was getting old, and though he checked out, apparently his heart just couldn't take the anesthetic Clark had to use to extract the tooth."

"I know Shazey was getting old. He would be twelve this month. Remember when we got him? Jack was so excited. He wanted a dog just like his best friend had. But he had to be old enough to carefully pick him up and handle him in general because of his long dachshund back."

"I remember," Jason said. "Every year on his birthday, Jack would ask if he was old enough now."

"Then, on his eleventh birthday, he wrote that letter. Remember how he explained all the reasons why he was old enough that year to have a dachshund puppy?"

They both started laughing, recalling that one of his reasons was that even his hands were bigger, so he wouldn't be as apt to drop him.

"Speaking of Jack, I wanted to tell you I'm so impressed with how he has matured. Graduating and working with you has brought out the best in him. I really enjoyed his visit and appreciated his help."

"He's doing well in the office, too—not as opinionated and determined that he knows more than the other guy."

"So, maybe we didn't do such a bad job raising him," Ellen said.

"I think his mother can take most of the credit for that."

"And now his father is taking over."

"I'm working on it," Jason replied.

Ellen was beginning to feel nervous. This was not how she expected their first meeting to go. "I bet you're tired," she said. "I made reservations at the motel we talked about. Why don't you go rest, have a shower, and come back in a couple of hours for dinner?"

"Good plan. What specialty are you serving tonight?"

"Pasta shrimp salad with your favorite dressing. Not exactly a specialty, but I look forward to it when there is decent asparagus at the market."

As Jason left, Ellen thought, "I could have been more gracious. I remember he really liked it, too."

Before Jason returned, Ellen set the table with the new dishes. Good-bye paper plates. She washed a bunch of grapes and got some corn fritters out to thaw. Then she went over her list of things she had considered they would discuss while he was in Land's End.

When Jason knocked on the door instead of just walking in, she thought, "Good, he knows this is my house. Having the renovation completed probably helped solidify that in his mind."

While Ellen brought food to the table, Jason wandered around the living area and commented, "I like the office being tucked in the corner. It's secluded and private but still accessible to wherever you happen to be."

"I really appreciate that, too," she said. "It's handy to the phone and information I might need when someone calls. After we eat, I'll give you a tour of everything we did."

"You had to have a good contractor. Jack said he got along very well with him."

"They seemed to, and I'm sure he also told you about his fraternity brother Stu solving the problem of finding someone who could do concrete counters."

"How's that working for you? Are you liking them as much as you thought?"

"Yes, they're great—no problem putting something hot on them and easy to keep clean," she answered. "Come and eat. Everything is on the table."

"Thanks, nice to have some good home cooking," he said as he sat at the head of the table.

"Hmm," she thought. "You can take the man out of the office, but he might not see himself as a guest at his nearly ex-wife's dining table."

As they ate, their discussion was easy and comfortable. Mostly about Jack, Jenny, their granddaughter, and of course, Shazey.

"Speaking of Shazey," Ellen said, "check the area under the stairs behind you."

It didn't take but a moment for Jason to realize that she had prepared a safe, comfortable place for Shazey to sleep. "Oh, I'm so sorry. You fixed a special bed for him."

"He was such good company and would have filled a place I've been missing. Maybe someday I'll find another Shazey." Needing to change the subject, she left the table and said, "Come on, I know you're curious about the changes."

"Good. I do want to see more of what you've done."

First, Ellen showed him the huge pantry, "I got the idea from my friend Anna, who has one the size of a bedroom in order to reduce the need for a lot of expensive cabinets and to make the kitchen appear to be more an addition to the living room rather than a place just to prepare food. I really liked Al's idea of open shelves in front of the addition. I have a clear view through it to enjoy my mom's garden and to let in more light."

Then they went into the addition. "Al built the cabinet to reduce the need for a coat closet and give me immediate access to a number of things like small hand tools, light bulbs, first aid kit, jackets, and umbrellas as well as a place to sit down and put on boots. Plus, it allows more space for the half bath and laundry."

"I'm impressed with all the thought you put into the renovation," Jason said. "How much did all this come to?"

Ellen felt taken aback by his question. She wondered, "Is he just curious from an architectural standpoint or concerned about my financial judgment? Or worse yet, does he think he should have been consulted?"

After a significant pause, she replied, "Not as much as I got from the sale of my parents' home. I know while you're here we need to talk about money, but I have another subject I'd like to talk about first."

"I feel I may have offended you. Sorry."

"'Sorry' accepted. I may have overreacted, too."

"No problem. What's on your mind?"

Even though Ellen had agonized many times about bringing up the David subject, she could think of no way to tell the story without involving herself personally. But the only reason for involving Jason was to get his input on what and how and when to tell Jack and Jenny. Finally, she began as briefly as she could. "This will probably be as much of a surprise—shock—to you as it was to me. In my dad's desk, I found a letter from Georgia Holiday, which told Dad about the son he had fathered. I met her and heard her story. Then, by chance, I met Georgia and her son David at the grocery store."

Jason suddenly stood up. "That's crazy! You must be mistaken. John never would have done that."

"I'll show you the letter."

"A lot of crazy women say a lot of crazy things."

Remembering her own disbelief when she found Georgia's letter and how Jason idolized her father, Ellen was able to calm herself and let Jason vent for a while. When the volume of Jason's voice decreased, she related the events more specifically. "Jason, my father didn't even know about David until a few years ago."

But no matter what she said, Jason couldn't seem to come to terms with his father-in-law having an illegitimate son.

Getting exasperated about the way the subject was going, Ellen finally interrupted his tirade. "I can see you're having a hard time dealing with the idea my dad had sex with anyone except my mother. But the only reason I told you about David is so we can talk about the effect it might have on Jack and Jenny.

You'll have to deal with your feelings another time." Ellen could tell that he was offended by what she just said.

"Why do they have to be told any of this fictitious nonsense?"

"Because, Jason, it's not a lie. It's not nonsense. And if it hadn't been kept a secret, we wouldn't have to deal with it now. If we don't, it's possible that Jack and Jenny might encounter it at some difficult time in their lives. Remember how close they've been to their grandfather and, like you, put him on such a high pedestal. I don't want them to be hurt, and I don't want them to think less of my father."

"Exactly. That's why we don't need to share something that would probably be hurtful."

"Land's End is a small community. Jack has already met both of David's daughters, who know Georgia's husband is not their dad's father. David knows who his biological father was. You can't assume that the girls would never find out that they have an aunt who lives only a few miles away from their grandmother. She knew it and never told them. Think of it, Jason. These are blood relatives. David is my father's son. He's my half brother."

The room fell silent. Ellen took a deep breath and then walked toward her room. Stopping at her door, she said, "Jason, why don't you go back to your motel and get some sleep. Maybe tomorrow we can talk more rationally."

"That might be wise. I can tell finding that letter had to upset you and was difficult for you to handle. I, too, have something I want to discuss with you. Thanks for dinner. See you in the morning."

Getting ready for bed, Ellen realized how tired she really was. Prayers for her feelings about David, her children, Jason, and what they were currently dealing with got all mixed up with the looming divorce. She was glad that God could straighten it all out. Soon darkness and peaceful sleep took over.

Ellen woke to the telephone ringing. "Good morning, Ellen," George said. "Hope I didn't wake you."

"No, just getting up for my first cup of coffee. What's up?"

"Do you remember the Albertsons?"

"Yes, what about them?"

"They invited me for lunch on Sunday and wondered if you could join us."

"Well, that was nice of them, but I have company right now," she replied.

"Maybe they could come, too. I don't mind asking."

Taking a moment to figure out what to say, Ellen decided it best to tell him, "My company is Jason." She noticed that George now appeared uncertain what to say.

Finally, he stammered, "Are you okay?"

"There are a number of things we have to resolve in order to get on with our lives."

With a sigh of relief, he said, "Of course. I didn't mean to pry."

"I'm sure you didn't. I'd better hang up. Please thank the Albertsons for me."

Jason arrived shortly after George called. Ellen thought he acted less disturbed but looked somewhat sheepish, likely because of his uncalled-for outburst the night before, which had made him appear immature.

"I'm sorry I upset you last night. I'm sure finding that letter had to have been more than just disturbing. How did you manage?"

"Two things—God and a good friend with whom to talk it out. Plus meeting Georgia and realizing that this had to be much more difficult for her than it was for me. Besides, she's a very caring person who by all accounts raised an outstanding citizen in Land's End."

"That's good to hear. When I was going over our conversation last night, I realized I had to stop thinking about myself, but darn it, Ellen. It's just that John was always such a Puritan. I mean, he never even told or listened to a dirty blonde joke. It made me proud to call him 'my father-in-law.' I just couldn't wrap my head around his having an illegitimate child. For a while last night, I was even mad at him, thinking this news might hurt Jack or make him think less of his grandfather. I'm sorry I reacted badly, and you're right about telling Jack and Jenny. I'd be mortified if they had witnessed my reaction last night."

"Maybe it was a good lesson for us. I remember a book club member of mine telling about parenting in the case of divorce. She said if a couple with children want a divorce, they can tear up the marriage license, but they will forever be part of each other's life if they care anything about those kids. So, they'd better learn to be respectful—at least civil—toward one another. That's what we have to always remember. Your children are my children, and my children are yours. And I know we want the best for them."

Jason walked over to the kitchen bar and sat down. "I know what your friend means, and I totally agree. A respectful attitude should be paramount in any relationship. I reacted too soon about the divorce, Ellen. I don't want to end what we had for the past thirty years."

Ellen recalled her conversation with Jack. "He was right. Jason doesn't want to divorce," she thought. Wow, wonder what happened. Why now? *Oh, Dear God, help me to listen, to understand.* No mere words could express her feelings. Hope? Fear? Uncertainty?

So, they both sat at the bar, allowing each other to absorb what had just been said.

Finally, Jason spoke. "Sonja is a very good architect. I'm lucky to have her in the office. But she falls short in so many ways. She doesn't bring to my life what you did. And I can't forget it. What do you think? Couldn't we start over?"

"You know what I always told Jack and Jenny. If you want an answer right now, it's "No."

Time passed without Jason saying anything.

Reflecting on their past two days' conversations, Ellen said, "I don't think you understand. Your affair hurt me, especially asking for a divorce just after Mom and Dad's accident, Jason. I'm sure now that you've had more time, you're

111

sorry about the breakup of our marriage. I'm sure you're sorry about how it affected our children and the apparent discomfort in your everyday life. But you really hurt me in a deep-down way that's hard to explain."

Jason broke his silence. "Do you think you could change your mind after you have time to think about it? I know Jack and Jenny would be happy to have their family back together."

"That wasn't fair," she thought. "Don't get mad. Stay focused," she told herself. Then she said, "I don't know, Jason. I've just recently started making a new life for myself—a new home, new friends, new community, maybe even the addition of some new family." Sliding off the bar stool, she added, "I think the train has left the station."

Knowing that nothing he could say now would make any difference, Jason walked to the door of the new addition. He thought, "But usually there's another train."

The End

EPILOGUE

Ellen continued to live in Land's End—a life filled (not unlike all of ours) with many ups and downs, but she found peace and joy with the help of God and many good friends.

In time, Jason retired, leaving the firm in the capable, experienced hands of Jack. Jason moved to the Pacific Northwest, where he still hopes to reconcile and spend his senior years with Ellen and get to know her half brother, David.